Ancient Sites of O'ahu

D1609816

Ancient Sites of O'ahu

A Guide to Hawaiian Archaeological Places of Interest

Revised Edition

VAN JAMES

BISHOP MUSEUM PRESS
HONOLULU

Native Hawaiian Culture and Arts Program

Ua lehulehu a manomano ka ʻikena a ka Hawaiʻi.
Great and numerous is the knowledge of the Hawaiians.
ʻŌlelo Noʻeau 2814

This project is funded under the Native Hawaiian Culture and Arts Program in celebration of the Legacy of Excellence of Native Hawaiian culture. The Legacy of Excellence volumes are devoted to generating an appreciation of Native Hawaiian traditions, art, and language through education, awareness, and recognition of excellence in Native Hawaiian achievement.

The views and conclusions contained in this document are those of the authors and should not be interpreted as representing the opinions or policies of the U.S. Government. Mention of trade names or commercial products does not constitute their endorsement by the U.S. Government.

Bishop Museum Press
1525 Bernice Street
Honolulu, Hawaiʻi 96817
www.bishopmuseum.org/press

ISBN: 978-1-58178-095-6

Cover image: Leina A Ka ʻUhane, a large stratified limestone outcropping, known as "the soul's leaping place" at Kaʻena on Oʻahu.

Photographs and illustrations by Van James, unless otherwise noted
Map revisions by Brad Evans

Design by Mardee Melton

Printed in China

Library of Congress Cataloging-in-Publication Data

James, Van, 1949-
   Ancient sites of O'ahu : a guide to Hawaiian archaeological places
of interest / Van James. -- Rev. ed.
       p. cm.
   Includes bibliographical references and index.
   ISBN 978-1-58178-095-6 (pbk. : alk. paper) 1. Oahu (Hawaii)--Antiquities--
Guidebooks. 2. Historic sites--Hawaii--Oahu--Guidebooks. 3. Sacred space--
Hawaii--Oahu--Guidebooks.
4. Sacred stones--Hawaii--Oahu--Guidebooks. 5. Oahu (Hawaii)--
History, Local. 6. Legends--Hawaii--Oahu. I. Title.
   DU624.65.J36 2009
   996.9'302--dc22
                                            2009011805

Dedicated to Kenneth Hōkūleʻa Ozaki and Lara Lindsey
Kasperowicz, their children Terrence Kahekili, Tyson
Laʻakea, Kalila Lehua Ozaki, Kiley Kawena Freitas, and
nā keiki o ka ʻāina.

Other books by the author:

*Ancient Sites of Hawaiʻi: Archaeological Places of Interest
on the Big Island*

*Ancient Sites of Maui, Molokaʻi and Lanaʻi: Archaeological
Places of Interest in the Hawaiian Islands*

Spirit and Art: Pictures of the Transformation of Consciousness

The Secret Language of Form: Visual Meaning in Art and Nature

Contents

Foreword

In ancient times, the sacred places of Hawai'i, or *wahi pana* of Hawai'i, were treated with great reverence and deference. These places possess spiritual power, *mana*, but the designation *wahi pana* means much more than just a sacred geographical spot. In Hawaiian culture, the idea of "place" itself holds deep meaning.

As a Native Hawaiian, a place tells me who I am and who my extended family is. A place gives me my history, the history of my clan, and the history of my people. I am able to look at a place and tie in human events that affect me and my loved ones. A place gives me a feeling of stability and of belonging to my family, those living and dead. A place gives me a sense of well-being and of acceptance of all who have experienced that place.

The concept of *wahi pana* merges the importance of place with that of the spiritual. My culture accepts the spiritual as a dominant factor in life; this value links me to my past and to my future, and is physically located at my *wahi pana*.

Where once the entire Native Hawaiian society paid homage to numerous *wahi pana*, now we may give *wahi pana* hardly a cursory glance. Only when a Native Hawaiian gains spiritual wisdom is the ancestral and spiritual sense of place reactivated. Spiritual knowledge and the *wahi pana* are ancestrally related, thus spiritual strength connects to the ancestral guardians, or *'aumākua*. My *'aumākua* knew that the great gods created the land and generated life. The gods infused the earth with their spiritual force or *mana*. The gravity of this concept was keenly grasped by my ancestors: they knew that the earth's spiritual essence was focused through the *wahi pana*.

My ancestors honored the earth and life as divine gifts of the gods. Their fishing and farming enterprises always included a spiritual function and focus on a *wahi pana*. Their activities never encouraged land or sea resource overuse because to do so would dishonor the gods. "The earth must not be desecrated" is a Native Hawaiian value.

The gods and their disciples specified places that were sacred. The inventory of sacred places in Hawai'i includes the dwelling places of the gods, the dwelling places of venerable disciples, temples, and shrines, as well as selected observation points, cliffs, mounds, mountains, weather phenomena, forests, and volcanoes. As my ancestral religion functions through a hierarchy of gods, practices, and lore, the *wahi pana*, too are hierarchical. A *wahi pana* favored by a dominant god or a high-status disciple is inherently more remarkable than one favored by a lesser god or being. The great god Kū is associated with the *luakini heiau*, or temple, while the lesser manifestation of Kū known as Kū'ula is associated with a lower order of fishing shrine.

The gods defined many *wahi pana*, but so did individuals, events, and functions. The south point of Hawai'i island, Ka Lae, is a *wahi pana* of long-distance voyaging and offshore fishing. Ka Lae served as a navigational reference for oceanic travel between Hawai'i and southern Polynesia, and priests communed there to use its *mana* in planning.

Though *wahi pana* are normally associated with geographical areas, this is not always so. For instance, Paliuli, a divine place of much spiritual presence, cannot be found with a map or jungle guide. Paliuli is discoverable only if one's mind and soul are ready to receive this *wahi pana* in the uplands of Hilo. Conversely, the water hole Palehemo, in the district of Ka'ū, gained spiritual status through functional use over many generations.

My ancestors and I believe in a life that integrates the world of the seen and the world of the unseen as complementary parts of a whole. My ancestors and I believe that a theme of *lōkahi*, or balance, is necessary for a healthy, natural existence. Both worlds are part of that theme, as are male and female, and day and night. Dualism was evident philosophically and physically in the life of my ancestors. *Wahi pana* were a part of this dualism, thus some *wahi pana* favor females, some favor males, and some are useful to both sexes.

I use the *wahi pana* in my practice of *pono*, or righteousness, which results in an increase in my *mana*. Use of *wahi pana* is most efficacious when the practitioner is a Native Hawaiian. *Wahi pana* rituals are usually performed when no uninvited guests are present; therefore, night and early morning ceremonies are typical. The rituals involve prayers, offerings, and conversations with deities. The rituals are closed because the ignorant often offend and desecrate rather than honor. Yet I have at times seen even foreigners, who have only read about the goddess Pele, bring acceptable offerings, such as food and foliage. The difference, of course, lies in individual sensitivity, thoughtfulness, and humility. These are the qualities needed to fully benefit from any *wahi pana*.

The *wahi pana* of O'ahu are part of my culture and values. These places need our protection and deference—not only for their historical significance, but also for their human significance. We Native Hawaiians offer to others many of the unique features of our culture, but sharing is not a one-way street. Any resource that is mined and consumed will become depleted if there is no attempt at conservation or replenishment. Overuse by tourists and the general public will result in the physical depletion of our sacred places and, subsequently, in the spiritual desecration of our *wahi pana*.

This guidebook approaches *wahi pana* with appropriate sensitivity, thoughtfulness, and humility. Those who visit and pay these sites the respect and deference they deserve, whether they are Native Hawaiian or not, will benefit from the experience of communing with the ancestors, learning the functions, and absorbing the spiritual power of the *wahi pana*. Study, observe, and appreciate, for these sites are part of spiritual wisdom.

—Edward L. H. Kanahele

Preface

My interest in assembling a guidebook on ancient sites of O'ahu is to encourage not only visitors to Hawai'i, but especially *kama'āina*, "children of the land," in the broadest sense of the term, to familiarize themselves with the remarkable legacy of this unique place in the Pacific. Precontact Hawaiian history is an important chapter in the story of humanity, and the sites illustrating this Pacific culture should be accessible so that they can be more fully appreciated and more clearly understood as markers along our journey from the past to the present.

Unfortunately it is rather difficult to gather information even on registered historic sites in Hawai'i. Perhaps the best known reference material produced to date is the Bishop Museum publication *Sites of Oahu*, compiled by Elspeth P. Sterling and Catherine C. Summers in 1978, which has recently been reprinted. This work and the research of other scholars in the fields of archaeology, anthropology, and Hawaiian studies was brought together for the first time in 1991 in an attempt to form a simple, readable, illustrated field guide to forty ancient sites on O'ahu. This has now been updated and expanded upon in the present revised edition of *Ancient Sites of O'ahu*.

This book is not an exhaustive study, although a broad sampling of resources has been drawn upon. The intention is to provide basic information about sites and guide readers to the sites that are easily accessible to the public. In some cases, permission or an entrance fee is required, but in all cases the sites listed are open or visible to all interested visitors.

It is important for more people to find that archaeology, ancient architecture, myths and legends, and even place names can add rich and fascinating dimensions to their understanding of Hawai'i. Reading, of course, cannot replace the experience of standing at a site and encountering with all one's senses the way a natural formation or a human construction is set within the elements. A *heiau* carefully placed on a mountain ridge, a *pōhaku* (stone) declaring its commitment to a particular place, a fishpond embracing scenic coastline, can only be experienced through a visit to the field. The intention of a petroglyph image, or the language of a rock formation, reads differently in nature than in a book, because its art and mystery are not yet trapped and funneled by the intellect.

Most of the sites included in this text are sacred to the Native Hawaiian people. The sites and their surrounding areas should be treated with reverence and respect; nothing should be altered or removed. It is important that visitors also leave nothing that may have an impact on the monument or the environment. In the case of *heiau*, which are sometimes places of burial, rock walls and platforms should not be climbed on or crossed unless an obvious path is provided.

When first visiting a site, view it from afar, considering the immediate impression it makes. Proceed up to and gradually meander around the site, noting its shape, structure, material, and placement in the surroundings. Where does the light strike it and how do the shadows fall? What form of landscape surrounds the site? What kind of vegetation is there? (Although the surrounding flora would have been quite different even a hundred years ago.) What views do you have from the site as you face the different directions of the compass? Most of all, what do you feel at the site? All of this helps to inform us about the *wahi pana* or sacred geography of the site.

It is sad to report that two-thirds of the known ancient sites on O'ahu have already been destroyed. However, new sites are continually being discovered and interest in saving the remaining sites is growing. Much has changed with regard to traditional cultural sites in Hawai'i since the first publication of *Ancient Sites of O'ahu* in the last century. Since then, new sites have become accessible while other sites have become inaccessible. Some site caretakers have changed as have visiting times and knowledge about the sites. This new edition includes ten additional sites and updated information on all of the sites. As with the original edition, this book is intended to promote the appreciation and preservation of the ancient sites of O'ahu.

Acknowledgments

I would like to thank a number of friends and colleagues for help-ing and encouraging me during the research and writing phases of this project. I am indebted to Catherine Summers for offering invaluable suggestions that helped lead to the format of the first edition of this guidebook. I would also like to thank Barry Nakamura, formerly of the Bishop Museum, who listened to my ideas and made helpful suggestions concerning a number of details. I am grateful to the staff at the Bishop Museum Library and Archives for their research assistance. Many thanks go to Ross Cordy, Tom Dye, and Carol Kawachi when they were with the State Historic Preservation Division of the Department of Land and Natural Resources, and to Earl (Buddy) Neller, formerly with the Office of Hawaiian Affairs. Many thanks to Martha Yent of State Parks.

Also, I wish to thank the many local contacts and friends who directed me to sites, accompanied me on adventures in the field, and aided me with information toward the completion of this work: Kalikina Akana, Nancy Ali, Sam and Mary Cooke, Chris Cramer, Michael Kioni Dudley, Patti Edwards, Edward Kepa Freitas, Rachel Ha'o, Malia van Heukelem, Roy Ihara, Chris Kasperowicz, Danny Kelly, Keli'iahonui Kotubrtey, Susan and Richard Lessa, Sweet Matthews, Diane McCoy, Mike and Dick Melcher, Alyssa Miller, the late Rudy (Lei Kaimana) Mitchell, John Morgan, Terrence Ozaki, John Pitre, Sigrid Southworth, Laura Thompson, Jeff White, and Robert Witt, many thanks.

I want especially to acknowledge the late Edward Kanahele for his Foreword, and the always helpful, David Kāwika Eyre, for his thorough attention to the Hawaiian language in the text and his contribution of the section on Hawaiian pronunciation. Thanks to Ron Cox for seeing the need for this revised edition and to Lan Tu at Bishop Museum Press.

My deepest acknowledgment goes to my wife, Bonnie Ozaki-James for encouraging me to take on this project, for typing and editing the original manuscript, and for offering suggestions, and going along on the search for ancient sites of O'ahu.

Ancient
Sites
of O'ahu

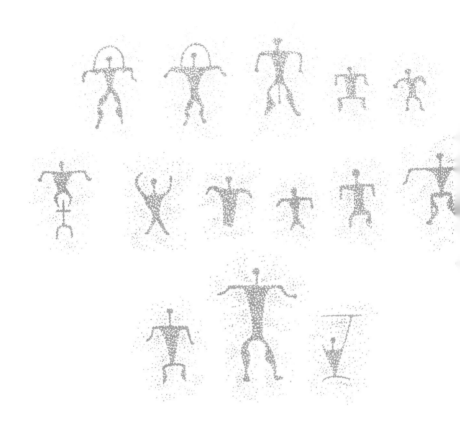

How to Use This Book

The first chapters of this guidebook sketch a picture of ancient Hawaiian culture and summarize the five major types of sites found on O'ahu. Fifty ancient sites are presented in the second half of the book together with site descriptions, location maps, and site photos. An overview map of O'ahu showing these sites appears on page 20.

The sites are grouped into five general regions of O'ahu. The sites of any one region can easily be viewed in one day of touring. In some cases, the sites of two or more regions can be visited on a single day. The East O'ahu and Windward O'ahu regions, for example, linked by the Pali Highway Tunnel, can readily be combined, at least in part.

If you are a visitor to Hawai'i, you may want to see more than one or two regions of the island in one outing: simply pick and choose sites by reading the descriptions and stop at those which sound most intriguing. Appendix B: Selected Sites for Visitors presents some easy options.

The "pick and choose" approach can also be taken by O'ahu residents who have the advantage of time. Read the descriptions and stop as time or circumstances allow to visit the various sites.

Alternatively, if you're interested in a specific type of site, such as *heiau*, the book can be used in this way as well. Each of the summary chapters on sites includes a complete list of sites in that catagory; consult the list and then look up the specific site description by title.

More serious researchers can use this book in conjunction with the books listed in the Selected Bibliography and noted as numbers in parentheses at the end of each site description. The first number refers to a specific title in the Selected Bibliography, the second is the page number in that work.

The Ancient Hawaiians

The ancient Hawaiians, like most indigenous peoples, felt an incredible rapport and connection with nature. They believed that the forces that caused thunder and lightning, or created sunshine and rainbows, were the same elemental forces that allowed them to stand, to walk, and to chant. These godly forces were so powerfully alive in the experience of the Hawaiians that they were recognized as beings and identified with names. Thus, not so unlike the people of ancient Egypt or Greece, the Hawaiians perceived a pantheon of gods, goddesses, and demigods as the sources of fire, water, and snow, and as dwelling in fish, animals, and plants. Pele, Kū, Kāne, Lono, and Māui are some of the gods still remembered today.

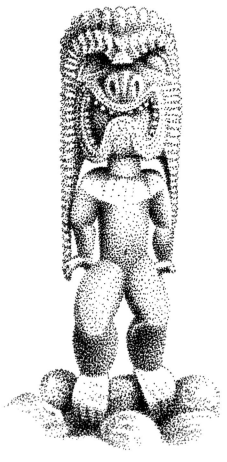

The ancient Hawaiian taro farmer, canoe builder, and fisherman, through his or her craft, were in constant discourse with the gods, for the gods were everywhere. Plants, soil, wood, stone, wind, and light all held more than just material significance for Hawaiians. Theirs was a meaning-filled natural world that instructed them not to kill the 'ō'ō bird for its yellow

Kū, god of war, was usually depicted in a threatening pose with toothed grimace and flared nostrils. Such *akua ki'i*, carved wooden images, stood within and sometimes along the approach to temple precincts. These images embodied the *mana* of the god or spirit they depicted; they were not taken to be the god itself, but rather a channeling post for divine intervention, similar to the ancestral totem poles of the Pacific Northwest. Few authentic *akua ki'i* survived the purging of the old religion that was carried out by the *ali'i* themselves in the early 19th century. This rendering is based on a late Kona-style wood sculpture that can be found at the Bishop Museum.

feathers, but to trap it, pluck two feathers, and release it to grow new ones. Their reading of "the book of nature" gave the Hawaiians a practice of medicine and art of healing far advanced in comparison to that of the westerners who in the 18th century "discovered" the Hawaiian civilization. Their deep understanding of the natural world order produced in them, for example, the knowledge needed to develop and manage fishponds for food productivity over many centuries. Their culture exemplified in some respects how the human community can enjoy a harmonious and mutually beneficial relationship with nature. However, this is not to say that life in ancient Hawai'i was ideal.

The *Kapu* System

The social order of old Hawai'i was very clearly defined. The *kapu* system set down strict societal "do's and don'ts," and the transgressor paid with his or her life. Most crimes were capital offenses, even fishing out of season, stepping on the chief's shadow, or eating bananas or pig (if you were a woman). Acquittal was possible for a *kapu* breaker if he or she could reach a *pu'uhonua* (place of refuge) and be cleansed and exonerated of the misdeed by a *kahuna* (priest). In times of war, the *pu'uhonua* was especially important as a refuge for warriors, women, and children whose side had been defeated in battle.

The *Ali'i*

The focal point of the Hawaiian social order and *kapu* system was the *ali'i*, the royal class. From this high-born group came the ruler-caretakers of the islands. They spoke with the continuous voice of their ancestors and were protectors of the gods on earth. Some ruled well and others not so well. Some would only go out at night so as to diminish the possibility of their subjects unintentionally breaking various *kapu* against them. Others took advantage of the *kapu* system, killing or inflicting suffering without reason.

Kamehameha the Great (1758–1819) is remembered as a powerful and wise ruler. He was responsible for uniting all of the islands' chiefly domains into one great kingdom under his leadership, but he was also the last to rule under the *kapu* system. Only months after his death in 1819, his favorite wife Ka'ahumanu and his son Liholiho abolished the old laws forever.

Kamehameha the Great (1758–1819) established the Kingdom of Hawai'i by uniting all of the islands under his rule. He was born in the Kohala district of the Big Island of Hawai'i; his name means "the one alone," or "the only one," and "the lonely one." (Based on a sketch by Ludwig Choris, 1816)

The *Kāhuna*

Chiefs such as Kamehameha had *kāhuna* as their advisors. These priests were not just spiritual counselors, but were political advisors as well. In many cases the *kāhuna* provided the actual direction and vision behind the *ali'i* class.

Hawaiian oral tradition speaks of Pāʻao, a light-skinned *kahuna* who came to the islands in the 10th century, some say from the mythical Kahiki, others say from Tahiti. Arriving on the Big Island of Hawaiʻi, he engineered the overthrow of the harsh ruling chief, Kamaiole. The lesser chiefs wanted Pāʻao to become the paramount ruler, but instead he sent to his homeland for a suitable *aliʻi* who could renew the Hawaiian royal class. Pili Kaʻaiʻea was brought to Hawaiʻi to become the new high chief, and it is from him that Kamehameha descended. Along with introducing the new line of *aliʻi*, Pāʻao also strengthened an emphasis on the war god, Kū, and probably initiated the practice of human sacrifice. Tradition also indicates that Pāʻao introduced the religious use of *kiʻi*, or images, as well as more elaborate *heiau* designs than had been previously known in Hawaiʻi.

A *kahuna*, however, might not only be a spiritual and/or political leader. A *kahuna* might also be a doctor, an artist, a craftsman, or a farmer. Specialists in many fields were in fact *kāhuna*. Long and disciplined training under a master was required to become a *kahuna kālai* (master carver), a *kahuna niho* (dentist), a *kahuna ʻupena hana* (master fishnet maker), or a *kahuna hoʻoulu ʻai* (agricultural expert). These skills and talents were passed from generation to generation, from master to apprentice, through internships that began often at a very early age and involved primarily imitation and repetitive practice. No books, charts, or other written materials were used in training the *haku mele ula* (master of chants and music), and yet thousands of lines of verse could be recalled and chanted. No compass, no sextant, no radar was available to the *kahuna hoʻokele* (navigator), and yet by reading the flights of birds, the size, shape and color of clouds, the wave movements, currents, and stars, this *kahuna* could safely guide his canoe, or fleet, through thousands of miles of open ocean (a feat doubted by western scholars until only recently when this science of navigation was reintroduced). Such disciplines as the *kāhuna* class had developed prior to the mid-18th century and western contact indicate a civilization that, although technically resembling that of a Stone Age culture, demonstrated very highly developed human capabilities.

Mythology

This direct relationship to nature was understood and orally transmitted by the ancient Hawaiians through living, imaginative stories—that is through myths and legends that told the tale of their culture. This traditional history presented the world in such a way that values, meaning, and morality were often of greater importance than, or at least equal to, the physical events being chronicled. These legends imparted the knowledge that physical objects were the result of creative deeds, and that facts were the by-product of godly activity. Thus Pele, the fiery volcano goddess, is credited with bringing the visual art of image making to the islands, because of the infinite form possibilities of lava rock structures attributed to her. She was considered the goddess of natural sculpture, an artist of "earthworks."

Ancient Sites

The various Hawaiian Islands were traditionally divided into land sections that usually included uplands as well as coastal areas so that the nature and people of these regions mingled and had access to the diversity of the different climates and resources within their land area. Such land divisions, which to some extent are still acknowledged as one of the most practical and ecological arrangements of land and sea resources, are called *ahupua'a*. The special characteristics and qualities of a geographic region defined its spirit of place. Sometimes translated as "storied landscape," the spirit of place or *wahi pana* tells us about the qualitative nature of a location.

The *kāhuna* accepted their creative skills and ability to experience the qualitative or "beingness" of nature as an inheritance from the *'aumākua* (ancestral spirits) and the *akua* (higher gods). Together with the *ali'i* and the commoners, they showed their gratitude and reverence by presenting offerings at shrines and *heiau*, and by worshiping before sacred *pōhaku* (stones) and wooden *ki'i* (images). What exists today as the ruins of ancient Hawaiian religious places, as well as the seemingly mundane remnants of aquacultural activity, petroglyphs, and the like, are but the bare bones of a once flourishing culture. Still, these bare bones of the archaeological record, together with mythology and traditional history, provide us with a glimpse into the rich cultural past of Hawai'i. They are the markers, focal points, or physical bodies for the beingness of the place.

Most of the ancient sites of the Hawaiian Islands are several hundred years old, according to scientific dating methods. As these methods are improved, the suggested time of settlement of the islands is continually pushed back. Recent estimates point to the 3rd century AD. However, neither dating techniques nor the archaeological reconstruction of ancient sites can be exact or final, as speculation based on limited evidence is often involved. What we consider to be true today is not what many thought was true yesterday or what may be recognized as true tomorrow.

This introduction to the ancient sites of O'ahu deals only with *heiau* (temples), *pōhaku* (stones), petroglyphs (engravings in rock), cave shelters, and fishponds of the island. Additional structures mentioned only in passing include house sites, animal pens, walls, agricultural terraces, irrigation ditches, wells, springs and baths, salt pans, pathways and roads, *hōlua* (sled) courses, and *pu'uhonua* (places of refuge). These latter sites are not of lesser importance, for all sites contribute to an understanding of the old Hawaiian culture; they simply lie beyond the scope of this book.

Types of Sites

Heiau
(Temples) and Shrines

A *heiau* is a Hawaiian temple, a place of worship, offering, and/or sacrifice. It is not only the most enduring architectural form from pre-Christian Hawai'i, but it is also the most important architectural form from the perspective of Hawaiian religion. As with most ancient civilizations, the temple architecture well represents and expresses the people and their culture. With an intense and immediate experience of the forces in nature and an intuitive relationship with their gods, the ancient Hawaiians looked to the *heiau* and their *kāhuna* (priests) for order, understanding, and guidance in the ways of the universe. This was the case right into practical everyday matters, such as ascertaining the times for planting and harvesting, fishing and refraining from fishing, healing illness and mending broken bones, giving thanks and being at peace with one's neighbors, going to war and taking another's life. The *kahuna* was responsible to the people as a mediator between the people and their gods. Each chief always had a *kahuna* to consult, particularly on questions dealing with the maintenance of power, and the *heiau* was the main center for *kāhuna* activity.

According to oral traditions, Pā'ao was the first priest to bring from Kahiki a new religious impulse promoting the gods Kū and Lono, but particularly Kū, a war god. It is believed that during Pā'ao's era, human sacrifice in connection with the worship of Kū superceded a more peaceful form of religious practice. Pā'ao is said to be the *kahuna kuhikuhipu'uone*, or architect, behind the 10th-century *heiau* Waha'ula and Mo'okini on the Big Island of Hawai'i, both of which were of the *luakini* (human sacrifice) type.

Kū and Lono, the latter who ruled over agriculture and was a god of peace, were already revered in Hawai'i at the time of the arrival of Pā'ao. Kāne, god of fresh water, and Kanaloa, god of the ocean, were also worshipped. There were also a multitude of other recognized gods and goddesses.

The line of Big Island chiefs, leading down to Kamehameha, stressed and ultimately spread the preference for Lono and the aggressive Kū over the other gods. Kāne'ākī Heiau in Mākaha is known to have celebrated Kū as its central deity during its later period, but its name could suggest that Kāne was the god honored there at one time. Some archaeologists believe Lono was the god presiding over Kāne'ākī before Kū became more powerful.

Only high chiefs, through their *kāhuna*, could consecrate *heiau* of the *luakini* type, where sacrifices ensuring the chiefs' power were carried out in honor of Kū. The preferred human sacrifice was a captive enemy, a warrior with much *mana* (spiritual power), *ali'i* having the greatest *mana*. A second-class sacrifice would be that of a criminal, and the lowest grade would be a *kauā* (outcast), a person considered to have no *mana* and capable of robbing *mana* from others.

Human sacrifice occurred late in the development of many ancient civilizations, and some historians speculate that human lives were taken in order to limit population growth. However, in Hawai'i, the *kāhuna* may have demanded human sacrifice in order to maintain a "fresh" connection to the *'aumākua* at a time when the spiritual vision of the *kāhuna* was failing and in need of help from a mediator.

Although human sacrifice figured in only a small part of the religious practices of the ancient Hawaiians, the *luakini heiau* nevertheless seem to be the most numerous and are usually larger in size than other types. This seems due, in part, to the tradition that only a few paramount chiefs held the privilege of establishing and using *luakini heiau*. Pu'u o Mahuka in Pūpūkea, Kāne'ākī in Wai'anae, and some think Ulupō Heiau in Kailua, served as *luakini heiau*, as well as for other functions.

At another type of *heiau*, known as the *lapa'au*, healers were trained and illnesses treated. Herbal remedies and spiritual healing gave rise to the ancient Hawaiian medical arts, practiced at sites such as Keaīwa Heiau, the most important site of this kind on O'ahu. The *heiau* surroundings served as the natural pharmacy for plant remedies of all kinds. Still practiced by some Hawaiians today, this natural approach to medicine was extremely effective until Westerners introduced pathogens against which the Hawaiians had no immunity.

All but the *luakini* type of *heiau* could be dedicated by lesser chiefs. Some of these other *heiau* were the husbandry type, such as Pāhua in Hawai'i Kai, where the promotion and increase of livestock and agriculture were fostered. The *heiau ho'oulu 'ai* were devoted to increasing the general food supply. *Heiau ma'o* were designed to promote rainfall and abundance in time of drought. Many *heiau* were quickly constructed over a period of roughly three days and used to fulfill a specific need, then abandoned. Sites were reused only if the need arose.

No two *heiau* seem to have been the same, as far as ground plan is concerned. Though often built on a rectangular rock platform, some *heiau* were terraced or stepped with two or more levels, while others were square in shape, and a few were even oval. It is only the stone foundations of these temples that we see today. Wooden fences usually surrounded the temple precinct

Pāhua Heiau (Site 13) in Hawai'i Kai is a ca. 14th-century agricultural temple foundation.

and grass huts stood within the enclosure. At some sites, such as Hale o Lono on the North Shore and Kāne'ākī in Wai'anae, these perishable structures have been reconstructed. One of the huts would have been the *hale mana* (place of spiritual power) or the house of the resident god. Sometimes a *hale pahu* (drum house)

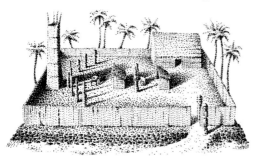

and an oven house were also present. Wood and *kapa* structures, such as the *'anu'u* or *ōpū* (oracle tower), stood near the *lele* or banana altar. Wooden *akua ki'i* (god images) guarded the entrance to the compound and watched over the altar. Although burials have been found within *heiau* precinct, a *heiau* should not be thought of as a cemetery in the contemporary sense. Burials were likely aids for a *kahuna* in his practice as a mediator between this world and the other, and often were only temporary until a cave or other more appropriate burial site was found.

Typical features of the *luakini* type *heiau* were, from left to right: the *'anu'u* or *ōpū* (oracle tower), which was entered only by the *kāhuna*; wooden *akua ki'i* (images of the gods); the *lele* (altar) for offerings; the *hale pahu* (drum house); more *akua ki'i*; the *hale wai ea* (house of the ceremonial *'aha* cord); the oven house; the *hale mana* (house of spiritual power) for the *ali'i*; and more images at the entrance of the precinct.

Little is known about the actual *heiau* rituals, as they were already being abandoned by the time foreigners arrived in the late 18th and early 19th centuries. Few first-hand accounts exist concerning temple procedures, though many second- and third-hand reports have been circulated. Samuel Kamakau, perhaps the most reliable native source, writing in the 1860s, said of the *luakini heiau* ritual that the human sacrifice, after being reddened over a fire, was placed face down with its right arm over a pig and its left arm clutching a bunch of bananas, outside the *hale mana*. A chant was then offered by the high chief:

> O Kū, o Lono,
> O Kāne, and Kanaloa,
> Give life to me until extreme old age;
> Look at the rebel against the land,
> He who was seized for sacrifice.
> *'Āmama*. It is finished.

Then the sacrifice was set on a *lele* before a line of *kāhuna* chanting a prayer in unison. The *kahuna nui* offered a prayer and everyone waited for its acceptance by the god, indicated by the sound of a bird, lizard, or other natural ocurence. This showed that "the ritual was freed."

The smaller, common places of worship were the *ko'a* (fishing), *'aumākua* (family god), and roadside shrines. These shrines were numerous throughout the islands and sometimes consisted of a single upright *pōhaku* or a rock structure the size of a small *heiau*. *Ko'a* were the most important small shrines, and remained in use long after more formal *heiau* functions ceased on O'ahu. The first catch was offered at such shrines usually located near the water. Some *ko'a* were sacred to specific fish and were believed to attract certain species. A *ko'a* might be one or more stones, naturally situated or artificially placed, often in an upright position and sometimes featured on a rectangular or oval rock platform or enclosure. Platforms of this kind, as well as most *heiau*, often contained bits of white branch coral, even if the sites were located at a distance from the ocean. This is one of the ways archaeologists can distinguish a *heiau* or *ko'a* from a pile of rocks.

It is believed that family shrines were an important part of every household. These shrines took the form of a single stone "idol" or an altar made up of many stones. Sometimes a special grass hut was built to house the *akua*, or guardian spirit; otherwise, the *akua* stood in the common living quarters or just outside in the open.

Road shrines often marked the boundary between one *ahupua'a* (land division or district) and another. There, travelers may have made offerings for a safe journey or left district tax payments, as was the custom. Today it is often difficult for us to imagine that a shrine, a sacred site, could be as simple as a single *pōhaku. (10/129–147; 13/257–268; 20/8–18)*

List of Heiau by Region

I   Kūka'ō'ō Heiau
       Pohukaina ('Iolani Palace Grounds)
       Pāhua Heiau

II   Ulupō Heiau
       Pahukini Heiau

III   Ahupua'a o Kahana
       Pu'u o Mahuka Heiau
       Ahupua'a o Waimea

IV   Keaīwa Heiau

V   Kū'īlioloa Heiau
       Kamaile Heiau
       Kāne'ākī Heiau

This *pōhaku* beside Waikalua Loko Fishpond in Kāne'ohe creates a *ko'a* (fishing shrine), marking the site as sacred to Kū'ula, the fish god.

Pōhaku
(Stones)

Many of the prominent stones and striking rock formations on O'ahu are sacred sites. A number of these sites have personal names and are the subjects of legends. This is because, according to tradition, they often represent individuals who were turned to stone, or they serve as the dwelling place for a specific spirit or god.

The *pōhaku*, whether it was a tiny *'ili'ili* (pebble) or a megalithic *pali* (cliff) boulder, was a very important part of religion in ancient Hawai'i. The features of the land spoke to the Native Hawaiians in a living, imaginative picture language and, therefore, the rocks and stones had names and being.

Offerings for the local deity were left at such *pōhaku* sites. Various forms of ancestral worship were also celebrated at these sites, especially when they were used as burial places. However, this does not mean that the *pōhaku* served merely as a gravestone in the conventional sense, but more as an altar-like marker indicating where an ancestor could be contacted. Some stones were used by the *kāhuna* in conjunction with spiritual practices, and others served as border markers for land divisions or districts. In this way, a *pōhaku* stood in the landscape as a physical reminder of both a spiritual and a physical threshold. In some cases, the ancient Hawaiians may have used *pōhaku* to measure the divisions of the year by reading its shadows, much like one reads a sundial, or aligning them to specific stars.

Still other *pōhaku* were known as *kū'ula* and were used to create *ko'a* (fishing shrines), marking a special fishing ground. Kū'ula was a fish god helpful to fishermen and lent his name to smaller-sized stones said to house his spirit. Often speaking through a dream, a *kū'ula* could direct a fisherman to such a stone's location and then, if properly cared for, could reward the fisherman with good fishing and a healthy life.

Some *pōhaku* were named after the objects that their shapes suggested, such as fish or animals. Jagged and porous stones were considered female; smooth, fine-grained stones were believed to be male. Usually, dark stones were male and light ones were female.

In ancient times, Hawaiians would leave fist-sized stones on top of their ti leaf offerings in order to prevent the leaf from blowing away. The strictly modern practice of wrapping a specially chosen stone in a ti leaf somewhat alters this tradition. *(7; 13/258, 260–261; 16; 20/19–21)*

He Ola Ka Pōhaku. There is Life and Death in the Stone.
—Ancient Hawaiian Saying

Fish god *pōhaku* from Hawai'i Island and O'ahu, now located in the garden of Bishop Museum.

Pōhaku Sites by Region

I Nā Pōhaku Ola Kapaemāhū a Kapuni (The Wizard Stones)
Pu'u Lē'ahi (Diamond Head)
Pōhakuloa
Pūowaina (Punchbowl)
Nu'uanu Pali Notches
Pōhaku Ka Luahine
Kohelepelepe
Kapaliokamoa (Pele's Chair)

II Pōhaku Pa'akikī
Nā Pōhaku o Hauwahine
Kānepolu
Mokoli'i (Chinaman's Hat)

III Kauhi'īmakaokalani (Crouching Lion)
Kahikilani (Washington Stone)
Pele's Followers
Pōhaku Lāna'i
Ka'ena

IV Hūpēloa
Kūkaniloko
Healing Stones of Wahiawā

V Mauna Lahilahi

Petroglyphs

Petroglyphs are pictures, and sometimes letters or words, carved in stone. The Hawaiian expression is *ki'i pōhaku*, meaning "stone image."

Hawaiian petroglyphs were simple in style and imagery, and remained that way even after contact with Pacific explorers, whalers, and missionaries. According to many authorities, Hawaiian petroglyphs did not have great cultic or religious significance beyond celebrating personal experiences or acknowledging the *'aumākua*. However, even with this more limited application in terms of religious expression, *ki'i pōhaku* were certainly a sacred craft as were the even more practical activities of mat weaving, wood carving, and tapa making. Stylized petroglyphs and the geometric designs of tapa cloth and tatooing represent the furthest development of ancient Hawaiian two-dimensional visual arts.

Ki'i pōhaku appear at over 150 sites in the Hawaiian Islands, but at only nine known places on O'ahu. The forms in these stone carvings are usually dots or cup marks, circles, straight lines, wavy or curved lines, as well as simple stick figures denoting dogs, turtles, birds, pigs, crabs, and human beings. Zoomorphic (human-animal) figures were produced, as well as figures on surfboards and canoe paddlers with paddles in hand. Sails and canoes are also represented.

Most of the Hawaiian petroglyphs were carved in lava rock, even in lava-tube caves. In addition, on O'ahu, petroglyphs were carved on the faces of large river boulders such as those in Moanalua Valley, and on coraline sandstone shelves along the older geological coastal structures such as at Kea'au on the Leeward side and Paumalū on the North Shore. (These latter two sites are covered by beach sand most of the year and are visible only when storm conditions occasionally expose them.)

Animal forms represent some of the images found as petroglyphs throughout the Hawaiian Islands.

Four different petroglyph techniques are apparent, varying with the sharpness of the artist's stone tool. Sharp tools produced pecked and incised designs; dull tools produced bruised and abraded designs.

Petroglyphs often served to indicate the beginning or end of a district or *ahupua'a*. Many ancient cultures worldwide have used markings between territorial regions. Ancient travelers were sometimes called upon to contribute to such sites by carving a figure as a kind of offering or acknowledgment of passing through the area.

Some of the Hawaiian rock art images, such as the Nu'uanu petroglyphs of dogs, deal with local mythology. Such dog images could be an appeal to the gods to ensure safe passage, or a warning of danger to unsuspecting travelers. A single petroglyph may have more than one meaning.

Petroglyphs of human figures, dot-in-circle, and cup marks can be found throughout the Hawaiian Islands. This group lies on private property near a destroyed *heiau* site in Hawai'i Kai (Site 12).

Hawaiian petroglyphs are not realistic illustrations of nature, but symbolic images of beings and forces. Figures are not depicted within a physical space: there is no ground line, no background, and therefore no foreshortening, no perspective or depth. The variations in the size of figures may imply rank or social status, as much as age and physical size. Groupings of figures can be difficult to read as compositions because individual units may have been carved at different times and for different reasons. Where a cluster of figures occur in a petroglyph field, the images at the center are generally the earliest, with later carvings taking whatever smooth surface area remained nearby.

Various methods of copying petroglyphs have been tried over the years, but such techniques as rubbing and casting contribute to the deterioration of rock art. The only safe way of reproducing petroglyph designs is to photograph them or to make interpretive drawings. Please help to protect all petroglyphs! (5; 13/271–273; 15; 20/21–24; 21)

Petroglyph Sites by Region

I   Nu'uanu Petroglyphs
         Pōhaku Ka Luahine
         Koko Head Petroglyphs

IV   Kūkaniloko

V   Mauna Lahilahi

Kūka'au'au Cave in Wai'anae.

Caves and Rock Shelters

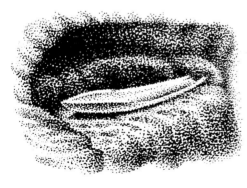

One type of ancient Hawaiian burial consisted in placing bones of deceased ancestors in the hull of a wooden canoe for their journey into the other world. These caves are *kapu* and off-limits to visitors.

Natural caves, lava tubes, and cliff overhangs were used by the Hawaiians as temporary dwellings and shelters. Fishermen often took refuge in caves and bluff shelters close to the sea, as the finds of ancient fishhooks indicate. The Hawaiians also sought longer term shelter in caves, as was true of most stone-age cultures. For instance, the Mānoa Valley Cave was said to have been the home of Kamehameha and some of his warriors while they were at war with O'ahu chiefs. Still other caves, such as Hilo Lā'au Cave near Kahana, were sacred and *kapu*, as they were the dwelling places of one or more gods.

Burial caves were also *kapu* and fairly numerous on O'ahu, where they were used by both the *ali'i* and commoners. A cave makes a perfect place for laying the dead to rest and for seeking communion with ancestral spirits: it is a space withdrawn from the eyes of the outer world; quiet, protected and dark, the womb of nature. In some Hawaiian caves, the dead were placed in canoes in order to help them on their voyage into the beyond, a practice similar to that in ancient Egypt of burying pharaohs with their bark.

Most of the archaeologically significant caves and rock shelters of Oʻahu are not included here as site locations because of the need to protect them. A number of them have not been fully excavated and others are on private land that should not be trespassed. The few cave and shelter sites that are accessible and can be visited are listed below. *(13/238–240; 20/32–33)*

Caves and Rock Shelters by Region

I   Hanauma Bay

V   Kūkaʻauʻau Cave
        Kāneana (Mākua Cave)

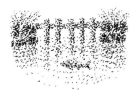

Fishponds

Fishing was one of the most important livelihoods in ancient Hawaiʻi. Besides fishing along the rugged shoreline and out at sea in canoes, a very sophisticated aquaculture system was developed using fishponds. Oʻahu had more of these fishponds than any other of the Hawaiian Islands because its irregular coastline of many inlets and bays made them easy to create. Though many ponds have been destroyed and few are now operational, close to 200 ponds at one time existed on Oʻahu.

Most of the island's fishponds were located along the shore, but some were also found inland. The Pearl Harbor area had an abundance of fishponds, as did Kāneʻohe and Moanalua bays. The Leeward side of the island had just one pond, in Waiʻanae. In the early 1890s, there were about 300 fishponds throughout the major islands, with 184 of them on Oʻahu. Today, about 25 fishponds remain, with only 13 of them operational or partially operational.

Ponds (*loko*) were usually built by enclosing a natural inlet or bay with coral or basalt rock walls and sand or dirt fill. The walls (*kuapā*) varied in size, but were constructed to prohibit flooding at high tide. They usually had one to four wooden *mākāhā* (sluice gates) designed to let fish in to feed but to prevent them, once well fed and fat, from getting out. Traditional gates or grates were made of *ʻōhiʻa ʻai* (mountain apple tree) wood lashed together with cords of *ʻie*, a woody vine. Half-inch gaps were left between

*Fishponds were things that beautified the land, and a land
with many fishponds was called "fat."*

—S. M. KAMAKAU

Mākāhā (sluice gates) were designed to let fish in to
feed but prevent them, once well fed and fat, from
leaving the pond. Traditional gates were made of
'ōhi'a 'ai (mountain apple tree) wood fastened with
a woody vine, leaving half-inch gaps between the
straight wooden slats.

the straight wooden slats. Most
ponds were salt water or brackish, but there were also inland
freshwater fishponds fed by
streams or springs. Where
fresh (sweet) water and salt
water mingled, in brackish
ponds, this was the ideal condi-
tion for producing a productive,
life-abundant fishpond. Some
of the most common fish raised
in Hawaiian ponds were *moi*
(threadfish), *'ama'ama* (mullet),
āholehole (silver perch), and
awa (milkfish). Ponds were also
home to varieties of shrimp,
crab, and eel. No ponds in use
today produce fish strictly
according to true traditional
methods without some modern
innovations, such as modern
materials. Modern aquacultural technologies are brought
to supplement and support
ancient practices today.

According to Hawaiian
legend, almost every water
resource, especially fishponds, were watched over by water spirits
called *mo'o*. These guardian demi-gods sometimes appeared as
beautiful women, sometimes as horrific monsters. Mythic descriptions portray them as lovely mermaid-like visions or as reptilian,
dragon-like creatures. They could be male or female, malevolent
or benevolent, but whatever their aspect they served dutifully the
body of water to which they belonged. Many of the fishponds
mentioned in these pages include tales of the local *mo'o*.

A caretaker or *konohiki* managed the ancient fishpond,
usually for the local or regional chief. People of the area were
called together for repairs on the fishpond or when large scale
harvesting of fish was necessary. Rights to the fishpond were
held by the *ali'i*. In the late 1840s, when the buying and selling of
land became official, all fishponds were awarded to Hawaiian
families, mostly royalty. But due to rapidly changing conditions,
the *konohiki* (caretaker) system weakened or fell apart entirely.
Fishponds were leased out, sold, fell into disuse, and in many
cases, were filled in and built over.

Because housing development, heavy vegetation, and the irregularities of the coastline tend to obstruct views of fishpond sites, it is often difficult to get a clear glimpse, much less be able to approach one. Only a few fishponds, the most accessible, are listed in this book for this reason. However, if you keep a sharp eye out as you explore coastal areas, you will likely spot the remnants of old fishpond walls, a sign of ancient Hawaiian aquaculture. *(13/211–214; 20/28–32; 27; 30; 32)*

Fishpond Sites by Region

I   Maunalua and Paikō Lagoon

II   Pāhonu Pond
Nuʻupia Ponds
Waikalua Loko Fishpond
Heʻeia Fishpond
Kahaluʻu Fishpond
Mōliʻi and ʻĀpua Fishponds

III   Ahupuaʻa o Kahana
Loko Ea Fishpond

Heʻeia Fishpond (Site 26) in Kāneʻohe.

The Island of O'ahu

According to Hawaiian legend, O'ahu was the child of Papa (earth goddess and mother of gods) and Lua (another husband of Papa after Wākea, god of heavens and light). The divine chief O'ahu was good to his people and they prospered under him. From a more physical point of view, O'ahu is the third largest island in the Hawaiian archipelago, and was formed from two volcanic mountains over a million years ago. The Ko'olau Range lies to the east and receives the brunt of the tradewinds with its rains, while the western Wai'anae Range, summits at 4,020 feet, the highest elevation on the island, and imposes an arid climate on the Leeward side of O'ahu.

When European explorers first made contact with the island of O'ahu in 1779, it was divided into six *moku* or large districts: Kona, Ko'olau Poko, Ko'olau Loa, Waialua, 'Ewa, and Wai'anae. These *moku* were further divided into smaller land sections called *ahupua'a*, which extended from the offshore reefs up to the major mountain ridgelines. O'ahu *moku* had between 6 and 31 *ahupua'a*. For contemporary travelers, this guidebook has divided the island into five regions according to their most commonly used English designations: East O'ahu, the Windward Side, the North Shore, Central O'ahu, and the Leeward Side.

Based on radiocarbon dating, settlement of the island was likely ca. AD 0–600, but no religious structures have been noted before AD 1000. During this early period, communities settled along the coastal regions and in the productive, wet valleys of the Windward side of O'ahu, only gradually making use of other areas. By AD 1300, most of the island was occupied with permanent settlements farming the lower valleys. Oral histories indicate an island-wide shift toward stronger religious and political organization occuring at this time. There were reputedly stricter *kapu* in connection with temple practices and chiefly status. Local chiefs ruled over small communities, while high chiefs controlled larger districts and, from the early 1400s, paramount chiefs reigned over the entire island.

According to oral tradition, La'akona was the first *mō'ī*, paramount chief of O'ahu, around AD 1420–1440. As population continued to increase, field irrigation, fishponds, house sites, and *heiau* appeared around settlement areas. Chiefess Kala'imanuia peacefully ruled the entire island from about 1600–1620, rebuilding *heiau* and constructing fishponds. After Kala'imanuia there was a period of unrest and splitting apart of regions. Around 1640–1660, Kākuhihewa reunited the O'ahu kingdom once again, and in 1720–1740, paramount chief Kūali'i spread his dominion out over windward Kaua'i and initiated warfare with Moloka'i and even Hilo, Hawai'i. During this time, a complex administration of O'ahu developed as intermarriage between the *ali'i* of the different island kingdoms flourished. Major *heiau* and fishponds were built or renovated during this era as the ruling chiefs traveled around the kingdom to oversee their people and lands.

Agricultural fields, fishponds, and settlements probably reached their maximum growth in the century prior to contact. The Pu'uloa (Pearl Harbor) area was renowned for its 36 fishponds and irrigated taro fields. The larger *heiau* were established by this time, and the Kingdom of O'ahu had an estimated population of 43,000 to 100,000 people. There were well-traveled trails around the island and across the Ko'olaus.

Around 1783, Maui's powerful paramount chief Kahekili convinced his nephew, ruling chief of O'ahu, Kahahana, to sacrifice his most capable advisor and high priest, Ka'ōpulupulu. With the great *kahuna* out of the way, Kahekili invaded and brought down the O'ahu kingdom. Kahahana escaped his fate for two years by hiding out in the mountains, but was eventually captured in 1785 and sacrificed at Papa'ena'ena Heiau in Waikīkī. Kahekili often used Waikīkī as his royal residence until his death in 1794, and he brutally crushed any and all rebellions by the O'ahu chiefs against Maui rule.

O'ahu, governed by Maui, was overthrown yet again in 1795, this time by Hawai'i Island's warrior chief, Kamehameha the Great. The culminating battle of Nu'uanu ended any chance of an O'ahu kingdom's return to power. As was the custom, the island was divided up and portioned out to the victorious Hawai'i chiefs and *heiau* were rededicated to Big Island gods. Kamehameha attempted two failed invasions of Kaua'i in 1796 and again in 1803–1804, but nevertheless effectively united the entire archipelago as the Hawaiian Kingdom. Like Kahekili before him, Kamehameha I settled part-time on O'ahu to rule his kingdom. Although the first king retired to Kona on the Big Island in 1812, and Lahaina on Maui briefly became the capital of the Hawaiian Kingdom after Kamehameha I's death, it was Honolulu with its protected harbor that could best serve the future needs of the Kingdom, the Republic, the Territory, and finally the State of Hawai'i.

The Kamehameha line ruled the Hawaiian Kingdom until the death of Lot Kamehameha V in 1872. There was then a series of elected or appointed monarchs until the overthrow of the kingdom and the establishment of a republic in 1893. In 1898, the United States of America annexed Hawai'i, and was attacked by the Japanese Empire in 1941, drawing the United States into the Second World War. The Hawaiian Territory became a state in 1959, with the capital seat and focal point of political and economic activity always centered in Honolulu.

O'ahu, the most populace of the Hawaiian Islands with about one million people, has been subjected to extensive development that has greatly impacted the ancient sites of the island. Still, numerous sites have survived and are accessible to the public (see Appendix A: Selected Site for Visitors, on page 135). While the meaning of the name "O'ahu" is unknown, the island is popularly referred to as "the gathering place." *(4; 13/106–121; 20/4–7; 28/ xi; 31)*

Map of Oʻahu

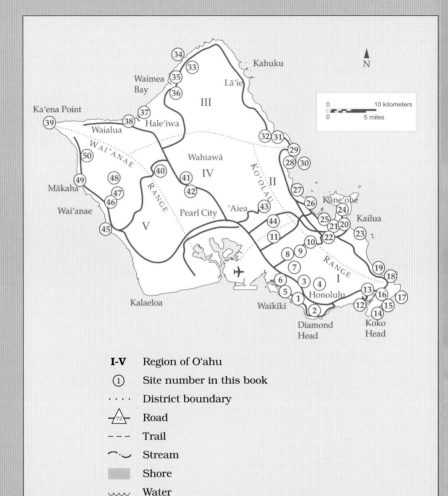

I-V	Region of Oʻahu
①	Site number in this book
····	District boundary
	Road
– – –	Trail
⌐⌐	Stream
▓	Shore
⌐⌐⌐	Water

Site List by Region

I. East Oʻahu

This exploration of the ancient sites of Oʻahu begins with the island's most populated area, Honolulu, formerly known as the Kona district. Approximately half of the island's annual visitors stay here in East Oʻahu, and a large segment of the permanent population resides in this area as well.

East Oʻahu has long had significance in the history and mythology of the islands. In 1845, during the reign of Kamehameha III, the capital of the kingdom was moved from Lahaina, Maui, to Honolulu. Major changes were initiated from the Honolulu seat of power, including the establishment of private property (the Great Mahele) in 1848 and the overthrow of the monarchy in 1893. Earlier, the unification of the Hawaiian Kingdom was in large part determined by Kamehameha I's conquest of the Kona region of Oʻahu.

Even earlier, in mythological times, it is told that Hiʻiaka made a journey through this part of Oʻahu on behalf of her sister, Pele, and the latter is said to have both arrived and departed from this easternmost end of the island. (Some traditions have her leaving from nearby Makapuʻu beach, others from Puʻu Lēʻahi.)

East Oʻahu has lost more ancient sites to development than any other part of the island. At least two dozen *heiau* were in this area, half of them located in Honolulu proper,

The Wizard Stones, as seen in the 1980s, before being rededicated Nā Pōhaku Ola Kapaemāhū a Kapuni (Site 1).

and seven of them situated in Waikīkī. For instance, the Lēʻahi Lighthouse and Hawaiʻi School for Girls at the foot of Diamond Head are both located on former *heiau* sites (Site 2). ʻĀpuakēhau Heiau, believed to be the oldest temple in Waikīkī, was located near the present site of the Royal Hawaiian Hotel, and Kapua and Kupalaha Heiau were both in the area of today's Kapiʻolani Park. Kūkaʻōʻō Heiau (Site 4), in Mānoa Valley, is the last remaining *heiau* close to Waikīkī and downtown Honolulu.

The East Oʻahu area has numerous burial caves and bluff shelter sites lodged in the southern end of the Koʻolau Mountains, the younger of the two Oʻahu ranges. The first carbon dates in Hawaiʻi were taken from a cave in Kuliʻouʻou Valley. In the 1930s J. G. McAllister, who did one of the first archaeological surveys of the island, writes of nearby Niu Valley: "Chief Justice Antonio Perry kindly directed me to the Niu cave. It is a tunnel approximating

100 feet in length. Near the mouth are remnants of numerous burials. Not far from the entrance is a wooden coffin which contains a few bones. Back of the coffin are fragments of tapas, cloth, lauhala mats, and portions of many skeletons. A small part of a canoe was seen. All of the burials have been disturbed." *(27/274)* This and most cave sites, however, are on private land and are not possible to visit. Only the Hanauma Bay shelter and the sea cave containing the Koko Head Petroglyphs are approachable.

There are several petroglyph sites in East O'ahu. The most accessible of these are Nu'uanu Petroglyphs (Site 8), Pōhaku Ka Luahine (Site 11), and Koko Head Petroglyphs (Site 15).

Koko Marina in East O'ahu was formerly home to a fishing village and a productive fishpond. Kuapā Fishpond, also known as Maunalua, had a 5,000-foot rock wall at one section of the pond. The area was presided over by the now destroyed Hawea Heiau on the foot of Mariner's Ridge, where rare, scattered petroglyphs and burial caves are also located. East O'ahu had close to a dozen fishponds at one time, including: the expansive Maunalua Fishpond (Loko Kuapā), Paikō, Kānewai (Kuliwai), Kalauha'eha'e, Kupapa,

Kamoana, Wailupe, Punakou, and other unnamed fishponds. For further information on this area, see www.maunalua.net.

From Hawai'i Kai to downtown, new sites of ancient O'ahu are continually being uncovered during construction projects. Burials in particular are regularly discovered at major construction sites in Waikīkī and downtown Honolulu.

Our tour of East O'ahu starts in the heart of bustling Waikīkī with the often forgotten Nā Pōhaku Ola Kapaemāhū a Kapuni (The Wizard Stones).

Nu'uanu Petroglyphs (Site 8), besides having ancient Hawaiian engravings, also displays grafitti from the 1860s.

Kanewai Fishpond (Site 12) in Hawai'i Kai.

Map of East O'ahu

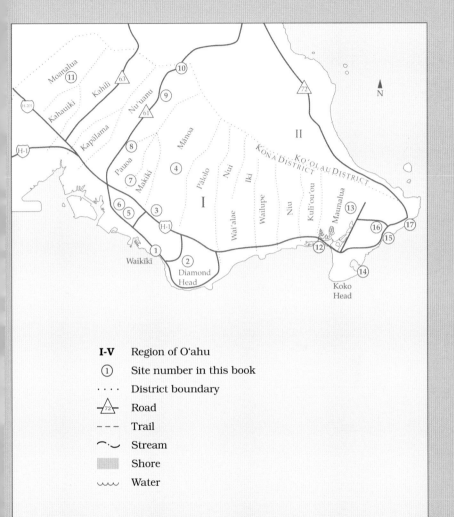

I-V	Region of O'ahu
①	Site number in this book
· · · ·	District boundary
Road	
– – –	Trail
⌒‿	Stream
	Shore
ᨑᨑᨑ	Water

1 Nā Pōhaku Ola Kapaemāhū a Kapuni
(The Wizard Stones)

Four large standing stones

LOCATION: Kalākaua Avenue, in Kūhiō Beach Park, next to the Waikīkī Police Substation.

These ancient stones, according to tradition, were once empowered with the *mana* (spiritual power) of four great *kāhuna* who arrived from Kahiki (the mythical homeland; some say from Tahiti or the Society Islands) before the reign of the 16th-century ruler of O'ahu, chief Kākuhihewa. These *kāhuna*, who became widely known throughout the islands as healers, instructed the people that four large stones should be moved from nearby Kaimukī and placed on the beach at Waikīkī. The stones were originally set in different locations: one was placed at the water's edge near the present Moana Surfrider Hotel, one was located on the 'Ewa bank of the 'Āpuakēhau Stream, and the remaining two were situated above the shoreline at Ulukou where the *kāhuna* lived. Kapaemahū, the head *kahuna*, named the larger of the stones after himself and imbued it with special powers. Over the course of a moon cycle, his companions, Kahaloa, Kaupuni, and Kinahi, did the same with each of the remaining stones. The four *kāhuna* then left Hawai'i for parts unknown.

It is said that in the late 1800s, Princess Likelike, sister of King Kalākaua, always placed a *lei* on each of the stones and offered a prayer before entering the water at Waikīkī. Governor A. S. Cleghorn, husband of Likelike, requested in his will of 1910 that

Nā Pōhaku Ola Kapaemāhū a Kapuni, the Wizard Stones, were so named because of the traditional understanding that they possessed healing powers.

the stones "not be defaced or removed." However, during the decades of development that followed, the stones were moved and broken a number of times. At one point a bowling alley was built over them. The sacred stones were rediscovered, moved to the water's edge, and then in 1980 placed in their present location at Kūhiō Beach Park. Here, beachgoers used them to sit on while waiting for the nearby public showers until a formal raised platform and fenced enclosure was created for them in the late 1990s. Known for years as the Wizard Stones, they were renamed Nā Pōhaku Ola Kapaemāhū a Kapuni by the late *kahuna lapa'au* Papa Henry Auwae in 1997. *(1/56; 7/33–36)*

2 *Pu'u Lē'ahi* *(Diamond Head)*

Extinct volcanic crater

LOCATION: Off Diamond Head Road between Makapu'u Avenue and 18th Avenue, opposite Kapi'olani Community College.

HOURS: 6 a.m. to 6 p.m., daily

ADMISSION: $1 for walk-ins and $5 for cars

According to legend, Hi'iaka, younger sister of Pele, compared the cliffs above the east end of Waikīkī to the brow of a yellowfin tuna, thus naming it Pu'u Lē'ahi. In the early 19th century, the designation of Diamond Hill and Kaimanahila stuck after British sailors discovered sparkling calcite crystals on the crater and mistook them for the precious gemstone. Now referred to as Diamond Head Crater, it is the most recognized landmark associated with Hawai'i. The 3,520-foot in diameter tuff cone, formed much later than the volcanic Ko'olau Range and rising 761 feet above sea level, probably went dormant less than 200,000 years ago. It was named a National Natural Landmark in 1968.

Pu'u Lē'ahi has long been considered a sacred place. On its western flank, facing Waikīkī, sat Papa'ena'ena Heiau until its destruction in 1856. The exact meaning of Papa'ena'ena has been lost, but one interpretation could be "glowing foundation." Here the sacrificial fires of the large temple would have easily been seen throughout the area. Descriptions of this temple vary but it is assumed that it measured approximately 130 feet long by 75 feet wide, with 6 to 8 foot high lava rock walls, 8 feet thick at their bases, and would have been open on the side facing the ocean. Papa'ena'ena was probably built by a paramount chief later than other Waikīkī *heiau* in order to consolidate and affirm power over lesser chiefs. Kahekili, high chief of Maui, may have built or renovated it in the late 1780s to commemorate his victory over Kahahana, high chief of O'ahu. This was perhaps his way of avenging the death of his ancestor, Maui chief Kauhiakama, who was sacrificed at 'Āpuakēhau Heiau in Waikīkī around 1610.

Kamehameha the Great also sacrificed at this *heiau*, putting the paramount chief of O'ahu, Kiana, to death here following the latter's defeat at the battle of Nu'uanu in 1795. Kiana's skull was displayed atop the *heiau* together with those of other defeated warriors. Kamehameha's nephew, Kanihonui, was also sacrificed here due to his intimate relations with Kamehameha's favorite wife, Ka'ahumanu. The affair was clearly not to the liking of Kamehameha I.

Walter Dillingham built his mansion, La Pietra ("the rock"), on the site of Papa'ena'ena Heiau in the 1930s in remembrance of the Florentine villa where he and his wife were married in 1921. It was built in a Mediterranean revival style with innovations by the Chicago architect David Adler, using local bluestone lava, pink stucco, and terracotta roof tiles. La Pietra has been expanded and is now home to the Hawai'i School for Girls.

Another temple was situated at the base of Pu'u Lē'ahi where the Lē'ahi Lighthouse now stands. Little is known of the now destroyed Pahu a Māui Heiau.

Access to Diamond Head State Monument is gained by a 580-foot tunnel on the eastern side of the mountain or by a steep hike up the side. Following the annexation of Hawai'i in 1898, Fort Ruger with a battery of canons was established within the concealing, protective crater walls. A four-level underground complex, bunkers, and an observation platform were built as a command post in the first decade of the 20th century. The complex is now abandoned but one can do a moderate 1.4-mile roundtrip hike through part of its unlit tunnels, and up its 175 steps to summit the observation platform for a spectacular view of Waikīkī and the entire southern half of O'ahu from Moanalua to Barbers Point. The crater floor is also shared by several government operations: the National Guard, the Civil Defence Agency, and the FAA Air Traffic Control. *(1/46–47)*

3 *Pōhakuloa*

Standing stone

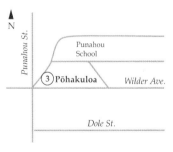

LOCATION: At the corner of Punahou Street and Wilder Avenue, in front of Punahou School.

Pōhakuloa means "long stone." The stone now standing at the foot of Mānoa Valley was apparently much larger in size before it was brought down from its original home on Round Top. It was said to have been a birthing stone, like those at Kūkaniloko near Wahiawā (Site 41), which blessed expectant mothers and endowed newborns with wisdom and strength. It was moved in the mid-19th century by permission of King Kamehameha III, and a large piece of it came to rest at the corner of Makiki and Beretania streets in what was then the garden of the Japanese consulate. Later, the first maternity home in the islands was built on this site, its location dictated, many say, by the stone's *mana*. Pōhakuloa was broken up further when Punahou Street was improved and widened. What is left of the long stone now stands at the Wilder Avenue entrance to Punahou School as a former boundary marker. An oral tradition tells of it being brought to the corner as a commemoration of the Great Mahele. A plaque affixed to the stone declares the school's name. The stone bears visible damage from its many moves and is held together in places with patches of concrete. Nevertheless, perhaps some "wisdom and strength" remains in Pōhakuloa and is passed on to the students of Punahou School.

It is said that Pōhakuloa has conversations with another stone that stands on the grounds of Punahou called Keapopo. The two stones call back and forth to each other: "Come over here!" "No, you come here!" But they apparently don't listen to each other.

According to legend, the neighborhood and school of Punahou received its name from a spring called Kapunahou. This water source was unknown until Kealoha and her husband Mukaka were both told in separate dreams that a spring could be found under a *hala* tree near where they lived. The spirit of the spring instructed them to make an offering of red fish, then pull up the *hala* tree. This they did, together with friends, and discovered a sweetwater spring that bubbled up from the spot. Kapunahou supplied enough water to generate a fishpond and maintain a *lo'i kalo*. A *hala* tree with taro plants in a spring is the logo for Punahou School. *(7/20; 12/18–30; 25/186; 28/283–284)*

4   *Kūkaʻōʻō Heiau*

Rockwork construction

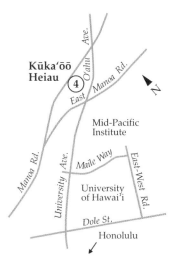

Kūkaʻōʻō Heiau is located in the heart of lush Mānoa Valley, where settlement may have begun before AD 1400 as a natural expansion of growth from the coastal area of Waikīkī. Mānoa was an ideal location for agricultural pursuits such as taro, sweet potato, breadfruit, and banana production as it was, and still is, a cool and water-rich valley. The *makaʻāinana* (common folk) farmed the valley floor while the *aliʻi* (chiefly class) preferred to live on the western slopes of the valley. Hawaiian royalty built retreats on these slopes, including Kamehameha the Great, Kaʻahumanu (who died here in 1832), and Kamehameha III (present site of Waiʻoli Tea Room). The location of Kūkaʻōʻō Heiau served both regions: the western slope and valley floor. Other Mānoa temple structures, now destroyed, were Puʻuhonua Heiau on Puʻuhonua Street, Kawapopo Heiau on ʻĀnuenue Street, Hakika and Hipawai Heiau.

The exact age of Kūkaʻōʻō is not known, for oral tradition attributes the *heiau* to Menehune (a small, dark-skinned race). Some believe the Menehune were the indigenous folk of the islands before the Tahitian migrations or a very early migration themselves. Others understand them to be elemental beings or nature spirits. Many of the older *heiau*, fishponds, and rock walls, especially on Kaua'i and O'ahu, are attributed to these legendary beings who were said to build large structures in a single night. The Menehune were paid one shrimp each for their night's work. Many stories about these little folk abound in Nu'uanu and Mānoa Valley where they were said to control the upper valleys. Oral tradition claims that they built a wall right across Mānoa and maintained a fortress upslope from Kūka'ō'ō called Ulumalu. In fact, Kūka'ō'ō is sometimes mistakenly referred to by locals as the Menehune Fort. Legend tells that the Menehune were eventually run out of the valley by chief Kūali'i around 1700. Kūali'i rebuilt and rededicated Kūka'ō'ō, using it as the central *heiau* in a series of valley temples. Another tradition holds that owls headquartered at nearby Pu'u Pueo chased the Menehune away.

Kūka'ō'ō is also connected in legend to Kapunahou, the spring at Punahou School (Site 3), through the story of a ten-year old boy and his twin sister who found shelter here. Kauawa'ahila and Kauakuahine (sometimes called Kauaki'owao) fled a cruel stepmother in Ka'ala and "hid themselves in a small cave on the side of the hill of Kūka'ō'ō." After some time, Kauakuahine longed for fresh water to bathe in. Kauawa'ahila spoke to Kakea, the *mo'o* of Kānewai pond, some ways away, who was also one of the boy's ancestor gods. Kakea magically provided a sparkling spring near the cave where there had not been one before; the spring was called Kapunahou and the area has become known as Punahou.

The story of princess Kahalaopuna, daughter of the wind and the Mānoa rain, should also be mentioned here. She was slain many times by her husband Kauhi, but was always brought back to life by her *'aumakua* (guardian spirit), the owl. Pu'u Pueo ("owl hill") is just across the street from the *heiau*. However, Kauhi was made to pay for his crimes by being turned to stone and facing up to the gods. From Kūka'ō'ō Heiau one can look across the valley to Wa'ahila Ridge and see the profile of Kauhi, Mānoa's Sleeping Giant. His head is *mauka* and his feet *makai*.

Based on its size and location, Kūka'ō'ō, was most likely an agricultural class *heiau*. Its name too suggests this function, as one of the god Kū's duties was presiding over agriculture and the 'ō'ō is a traditional digging stick. So "god of the digging stick" is a possible translation. A second translation is derived from an oral tradition that tells of Kawelokamahamahai'a, from Kaua'i, who came over to O'ahu and stood on Mānoa's highest peak, Konahuanui. From there he threw his pronged spear, resembling an 'ō'ō, that stuck upright (*kū*) in the ground at the *heiau* site. Thus, Kūka'ō'ō, "the upright digging stick." As an agricultural *heiau* it would have been used to promote crop growth through ritual practice and offerings of first crops.

Kūka'ō'ō Heiau is a small terraced rock structure above a short, steep slope. The outer dimensions of the temple are about 50 by 40 feet. There is an enclosure with a 5-foot wide opening in the western corner. Some reinforced walls are 3 feet thick and the highest wall is 9 feet tall. During restoration it was discovered that the main wall was originally constructed with three layers of stone for structural strength. An oval feature was also uncovered near the *heiau* entrance, and has been retained. Kūka'ō'ō Heiau was cleared of over growth and restored in the 1990s.

Kūka'ō'ō Heiau stands directly behind the historic Cooke home, Kūali'i, which will eventually become a museum.

The *heiau* stands behind the Sam and Mary Cooke house, built by Charles Montague Cooke Jr. in 1911 by the architects Emory and Webb, who also designed Hawai'i Theatre and the Wai'oli Tea Room. The architects originally wanted to build on the *heiau* site itself but landowner "Monty" Cooke insisted on preserving the temple. Done in a Tudor revival style, using volcanic basalt rock quarried at the site, the house was named Kūali'i, after the historic local chief. The house, *heiau*, and grounds (landscaped with native plants) are on the National Register of Historic Places. The main house, Kūali'i, and the Cooke's collection of quality art and artifacts, will eventually become a museum.

Kūka'ō'ō Heiau is cared for by the Mānoa Heritage Center, a non-profit organization founded in 1996, whose mission is to promote the stewardship of the natural and cultural heritage of Hawai'i, and specifically to preserve and interpret the *heiau*, gardens, historic home, and Mānoa Valley. *(12/18–30; 20, 27/285–289)*

NOTE: Reservations must be made to visit this site. Walk-ins will be turned away.

PHONE: (808) 988-1287, for reservations and directions.

WEBSITE: www.manoaheritagecenter.org

HOURS: 9 a.m. to 4 p.m., Tuesdays to Saturdays

ADMISSION: Adults $7; senior/military $4; children/students free (regardless of age). Advance reservations required.

5   Ka Wai a Ha'o

Sacred spring

**LOCATION: 957 Punchbowl Street
at the corner of South King
Street across from Honolulu Hale
(City Hall).**

Prior to its settlement in the 19th century, this area just outside the village of Honolulu was dry and barren apart for a small verdant spot with a spring reserved for *ali'i*, high chiefs and chiefesses. One visitor to the *kapu* spring was the chiefess Ha'o. She was regularly carried to the sacred spring from her home in Mō'ili'ili for ceremonial bathing and purifying in its waters. One source says that Ha'o was a chief, and a member of the lineage is buried in the nearby church cemetery. Eventually the sweetwater pool and its surrounding oasis became known as Ka Wai a Ha'o, "the water of Ha'o."

When the first missionaries arrived from New England in 1920, they found favor with the royalty and were granted land at Ka Wai a Ha'o. They built homes where the present Mission Houses Museum now stands and a thatched, Hawaiian-style sanctuary, measuring 54 feet by 22 feet, where the Kawaiaha'o Church stands. Three more thatched churches were erected over the succeeding years until the present "Great Stone Church," as it was called then, was built. In fact Kawaiaha'o Church is not built of stone, but is constructed of 14,000 coral blocks, weighing 1,000 pounds each. Hand-chiseled from the living reef in coastal waters 10 to 20 feet deep, the entire project took five years to complete. On

July 21, 1842, dedication ceremonies for the church took place with King Kamehameha III, a generous supporter of the project, in attendance. It wasn't until 1853 that the sanctuary was called Kawaiaha'o. The tower clock was donated by the king and named Kauikeaouli, after him, and still operates on the original machinery. Kawaiaha'o has a long history with the Hawaiian monarchy as royal marriages and coronations took place here as did many other important events. Kamehameha III is said to have uttered here the words that became the state motto: *Ua mau ke ea o ka 'āina i ka pono*, the life of the land is preserved in righteousness. William Charles Lunalilo, the sixth king of Hawai'i, preferred to be buried on the church grounds "near his people," rather than at the Royal Mausoleum in Nu'uanu. His Gothic revival style mausoleum is directly in front of the church. Just inside Kawaiaha'o Church are pews reserved for Hawaiian royalty and they are still used today.

The sacred spring of Ka Wai a Ha'o was actually closer to the present intersection of South King and Kapi'olani Streets. The present artificial pool, with piped-in water, was built beside Kawaiaha'o Church in 1926. However, it does incorporate one of the original stones from the ancient spring of Ka Wai a Ha'o. *(25/97)*

6 *Pohukaina* *('Iolani Palace Grounds)*

Historic building and burial mound

LOCATION: **364 South King Street at the corner of Richard Street in downtown Honolulu.**

PHONE: **(808) 522-0822**

WEBSITE: **www.iolanipalace.org**

HOURS: **9 a.m. to 11:15 a.m. Guided tours, $20. 11:15 a.m. to 3:30 p.m. Audio tours, $13. Mondays through Saturdays.**

ADMISSION: **Palace entry is $6 adults; $3 children; access to the grounds is free.**

The grounds of 'Iolani Palace are believed to be the site of the now destroyed Ka'ahaimauli Heiau, and the burial cave, Pohukaina ("the calm and quiet land"), is said to have been located here as well. Stories tell of the cave extending to several distant locations on O'ahu, including Kāneana, Makua Cave (Site 50). It was here in 1825 that a small, 10 foot high, 18 foot wide by 24 foot long, Western-style, whitewashed coral block structure was built as the royal tomb for Kamehameha II and his consort, Queen Kamāmalu. The year before, while in England to consolidate an alliance between Hawai'i and Great Britain, the royal couple died of measles. Until 1865 other Hawaiian kings and queens were also buried here, making it the official royal tomb. However, during the reign of King Kamehameha IV and Queen Emma, a solemn torchlit procession removed eighteen royal coffins and brought them to Mauna 'Ala (Fragrant Hills), the new Royal Mausoeleum in Nu'uanu Valley, built for their recently deceased son Prince Albert. The present mound on the 'Iolani Palace grounds is a symbolic marker of the former *kapu* (sacred) resting place of royalty. Some assert that the mound retains not only the

The 'Iolani Palace coat of arms depicts two *ali'i* flanking the royal crown and crest. The accompanying motto was uttered by King Kamehameha III on the occasion of the restoration of the Hawaiian Kingdom by the British: *Ua mau ke ea o ka 'āina i ka pono,* "The life of the land is perpetuated in righteousness."

mana of the former site, but also actual remains as well. Remember, this sacred mound should be respected and not trespassed. William Charles Lunalilo, the sixth king of Hawai'i, is buried directly across the street on Kawaiaha'o Church grounds (Site 5) in order to be "near his people," and distanced himself from the Kamehameha family remains interred at the Royal Mausoleum in Nu'uanu.

It was here, beside the original tomb, that King Kamehameha III established his official Honolulu residence in 1845. The monarch built a large wooden home that served five Hawaiian kings until its demolition in 1874 to make way for 'Iolani Palace. The original palace was known as Hale Ali'i (House of the Chief). However, in honor of his brother and predecessor, King Kamehameha V, he renamed the site 'Iolani. '*Io* is the Hawaiian hawk, the highest flying of birds, and *lani* means "heavenly" or "exalted." Directly across the street from 'Iolani Palace is Ali'iōlani Hale (House of the Heavenly Chief), originally designed as a royal palace for King Kamehameha V, who died before its completion in 1874. It is presently the Hawai'i State Supreme Court and administrative offices for the Hawai'i State Judiciary.

The palace grounds were at first surrounded by an 8-foot high coral block wall, but following the Wilcox Rebellion in 1889, the wall was lowered to 3.5 feet. The present painted ironwork fence on top was added in 1891. The four principle gates to the palace grounds bear the coat-of-arms of the Hawaiian Kingdom,

Offerings are often left at an *ahu* beside the burial mound on the grounds of 'Iolani Palace.

and are named for Hawaiian royalty. They served different purposes: Kauikeaouli—Kamehameha III, the main gate in the south, was used for ceremonial occasions; Kīna'u—mother of Kamehameha IV, the western, Richard Street gate was used by tradesmen; Hakaleleponi—Queen Kalama, consort of Kamehameha III, faces the present Hawai'i State Capitol in the north and was used by servants of the royal household; Likelike—princess sister of King Kalākaua and Queen Lili'uokalani, was the east private entrance for the royal family. The coat-of-arms depicts two *ali'i* in traditional feather capes and headdresses flanking the royal crown and crest. The motto upon which the figures stand was uttered by King Kamehameha III on the occasion of the restoration of the Hawaiian Kingdom by the British: *Ua mau ke ea o ka 'āina i ka pono,* "The life of the land is perpetuated in righteousness."

Also within the palace grounds are: Halekoa, the barracks of the Royal Guard, completed in 1871, and moved from its original site on the grounds of the Hawai'i State Capitol in 1965; Keli'iponi, the Coronation Pavilion, built in 1883 for the coronation of King Kalākaua and Queen Kapi'olani; the Kana'ina Building or Old Archives, built in 1906; and, of course, the 'Iolani Palace itself.

The 'Iolani Palace cornerstone was laid in 1879 with full Masonic rites, using rock from Kūki'i Heiau on the southeastern corner of the Big Island. It was completed as a modern, world-class building in 1882. King David Kalākaua, the first king to visit the United States and to circumnavigate the globe, saw to it that his palace was up-to-date and even in advance of its time with indoor plumbing, inter-room telephones, and electric lighting (before the White House). King Kalākaua was known as the "Merrie Monarch" because of his enthusiasm for culture and the arts. He was himself an avid musician and he encouraged the transcription of Hawaiian oral traditions. He was responsible for the revival of public performances of *hula* and chanting, which had been banned by the missionaries, and the revival of *lua,* the Hawaiian martial arts, and surfing. 'Iolani Palace is the only royal palace within the United States. *(26/56–57, 187; 31)*

7 *Pūowaina* *(Punchbowl)*

Extinct volcanic crater

LOCATION: 2177 Pūowaina Drive, Honolulu, HI 96813-1729

PHONE: (808) 532-3720

HOURS: 8:00 a.m. to 6:30 p.m., daily

Pūowaina means "hill of sacrifice," for in ancient times Hawaiians made human sacrifices at this natural altar at the foot of the Ko'olau Mountains in order to appease the gods of the ruling chiefs. Anyone who broke one of the strict traditional laws could be burned on the *imu ahi*, oven fire, set up on the rim of this volcanic crater hill. Sacrificed bodies were placed on a large stone at the crater's edge and a powerful updraft created a fire that quickly consumed the offering. The altar stone was located where the present overlook is situated, but has since disappeared. *Kapu* breakers were actually put to death at Kewalo Basin, down at the ocean side where there was a fishpond and a spring called Kawailumalumai, "drowning waters." Victims were prepared for death by a *kahuna* priest who instructed them to, "Lie still [die] in the waters of your chief." The lifeless body would then be ceremoniously carried past Manu'a Heiau (the Queen's Hospital site), home of the high priest, up to Kanela'au/Po'ouahi Heiau (the site of Robert Louis Stevenson School) just beside the crater for further rites before proceeding to the altar fire at Pūowaina's Puhi Kanaka Heiau. The last known human sacrifice to be offered at Pūowaina was in 1809.

Samuel Kamakau, the 19th-century Native Hawaiian historian, tells us that the legendary Menehune lived on Pūowaina. At one time, much of the region around the crater was terraced and cultivated with sweet potato. A *hōlua* slide ran down the southern slope toward Waikīkī and provided the fastest land speed experiences to *ali'i* that dared this *kapu* sport. It was used during the rainy season when the ground was damp and slippery, usually at midday when there were no shadows.

A natural fortification, Pūowaina, better known as Punchbowl, was formed between 75,000 and 100,000 years ago, and is believed to be younger than Pu'u Lē'ahi (Diamond Head). The first major battle for the unification of all the islands took place here between O'ahu warriors and the invading Hawaiian armies in 1795. Fighting raged along a series of *heiau* that led up to Kanela'au Heiau. Overwhelmed, the O'ahu forces fled through the crater and up to the Nu'uanu Pali where they were eventually defeated. Kamehameha I later placed a pair of canons on the crater to salute foreign ships, and six more were installed in 1816 when fears of a Russian invasion were rumored. Following the overthrow of the Hawaiian monarchy, canons were fired from Punchbowl against Royalists attempting to take Pūowaina in 1895. The queen's guard, leading the advance, surrendered after fifteen rounds were fired from the crater's battery. Then, fortified with modern guns, Punchbowl was prepared at the beginning of World War II for a possible sea invasion, but was entirely useless against an air strike.

Today, Pūowaina is the site of the National Memorial Cemetery of the Pacific and the resting place of nearly 50,000 service men and

women who sacrificed their lives for their country. The 111.5-acre cemetery honors soldiers from the Boxer Rebellion, World War II, the Korean Conflict, and the Vietnam War, as well as two Hawai'i born astronauts. It was first recommended as a cemetery in the 1890s for the growing population of Honolulu, but nothing became of it because of fears that a city of the dead above a city of the living was bad luck. In 1943, the territorial governor of Hawai'i offered Punchbowl to

An Ashes Scattering Site is still used for military funeral services on the southeast rim of Pūowaina, at Punchbowl National Memorial Cemetery of the Pacific.

the military for a cemetery site. However, it took until 1949 (thousands of bodies were stored in warehouse mortuaries on Guam following WWII) before the first remains from the Pacific war were interred and it officially became a cemetery. There is an Ashes Scattering Site that is still used for military funeral services located near the original spot where ancient Hawaiian sacrifices took place. The Punchbowl National Memorial Cemetery of the Pacific was placed on the National Register of Historic Places in 1976, and it continues to live up to its name, Pūowaina. *(28/291–292)*

8 *Nu'uanu Petroglyphs*

Petroglyphs on natural rock walls

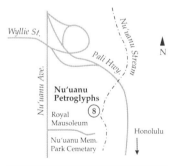

LOCATION: Along the west bank of Nu'uanu Stream behind the Nu'uanu Memorial Park Cemetery and Royal Mausoleum. An easy hike just above the streambed is required to reach the site.

Numerous carved animal and human figures can be found at three separate sites in the immediate vicinity of Alapena Pool below Kapena Falls. The easiest of these sites to find is the "man and dog" petroglyphs that can be seen along the trail west of Nu'uanu Stream at Nu'uanu Memorial Park. The figures are engraved on a rock wall now enclosed by a protective iron grating. Beside this site are numerous, engraved historic names and dates from the 19th century.

The two other petroglyph sites, also located on the west bank south of Alapena Pool, have in total as many as forty carved units, mostly human and animal figures.

In one interpretation, the dog images may refer to the legendary guardian dog of Kapena Falls. This dog protected people from harm and was believed to be a *kupua*, a supernatural creature who could take on various forms. In one legend, the guardian dog Kaupe saves a traveler from death at the hands of robbers. However, interpretation of the Nu'uanu Petroglyph figures remains uncertain. *(5; 13/116; 16; 20/83–84; 21; 28/299–300)*

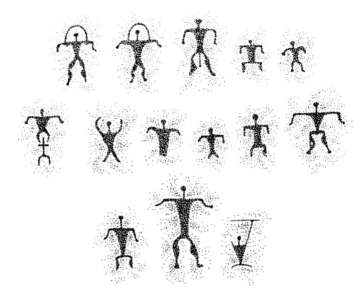

These three rows of figures are from the three separate sites collectively known as the Nuʻuanu Petroglyphs. Located in the immediate vicinity of Alapena Pool, these selected human figures are probably of a later date than the plain stick figure or simple outline types found elsewhere in Hawaiʻi. Details such as muscles, fists, and feet indicate greater self-consciousness, clearer observation of physical characteristics, and heightened artistic skill. Note the halo around the so-called "rainbow warrior."

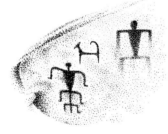

A carving at one of the Nuʻuanu Petroglyph sites clearly represents the figure of a dog standing over the shoulder of a human form. These images are not of the early stick-figure type, but of a more filled-in, muscular style that indicates they may be of a later date. The dog figures prominently in Nuʻuanu Valley lore as a guardian spirit, a *kupua* or supernatural shape-changing being.

An old photo of the Nuʻuanu Petroglyphs shows numerous dog and human figures. (Bishop Museum Archives)

9 *Kaniakapūpū*

Historic ruin

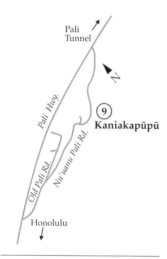

Pali Tunnel

Pali Hwy.

N

⑨ Kaniakapūpū

Old Pali Rd.

Nu'uanu Pali Rd.

Honolulu

LOCATION: Nu'uanu Pali Drive, opposite side of road and 100 yards *mauka* of the Board of Water Supply building. Take the trail into the bamboo forest and bear left off the straight path after 100 yards. Permission from the Board of Water Supply is recommended.

This site was originally home to Kaniakapūpū Heiau, now destroyed. The extent of this temple is unknown, but it was said to have served two purposes. As a healing center or *heiau ho'ōla*, like Keaīwa Heiau in 'Aiea (Site 43), it supported the work of *kāhuna lapa'au*, medicine men and women. Travelers would stop here on there way over the Pali for relaxing and healing and in return offered a tithing to the priests. The area is also called Luakaha, "place of relaxation." During his conquest of O'ahu, Kamehameha I rested his warriors at this place. The *heiau* is reported to have been dedicated to Lono, an agricultural god. The area was known for its shells, and Kaniakapūpū means "song of the land shells."

Kauikeaouli, Kamehameha III, used this *kapu* (sacred) site to build his summer palace, and called it Kaniakapūpū after the *heiau*. It was here that he retired to during the hot months of the year to hold court as well as to entertain. At one party he hosted in 1847, there were apparently 10,000 guests present, all of whom were entertained and fed well. Early reports sometimes refer to the place as "His Majesty's county seat," and it may be from here that the Mahele, the right to buy and sell property, was planned.

It was also here that Kamehameha IV was educated in the ways of the world. An early chronicler states: "For the future king was educated in two ways. First he was trained to be a king in the western style. And then he was brought up here to the valley to his father's palace and trained as a Hawaiian chief."

The palace itself was a large rectangular structure with one room and porch around the outside. There was a cookhouse to the left side of the main building and numerous thatched *hale* would have complimented the complex. The ancient *heiau* was to the right and behind the palace. By 1874 the site was described as an "old ruin." Today it is more so. It sits on watershed land and permission to access the property is required.

Other destroyed or inaccessible Nu'uanu *heiau* are Kaheiki, Kawaluna, Kupuanuu, Kupualani, Paka'alanalalo, Luna, and Makuku Heiau. *(28/307–309)*

This possible cookhouse to the left of the main building would have been one of the auxillary structures at the Kaniakapūpū complex.

10 *Nu'uanu Pali Notches*

Artificially modified mountain ridge

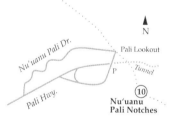

Pali Lookout

P *Tunnel*

⑩
Nu'uanu
Pali Notches

LOCATION: In Nu'uanu Pali State Park, off Pali Highway, route 61, between Honolulu and Kailua. You can see the cliff-top notches from the Pali Highway as you approach from Honolulu before entering the park, and from the Kailua side from various vantage points.

Nu'uanu means "cool terrace" or "cool heights," and it is in this upper valley that the great battle took place that ensured the future unification of the islands under the authority of Kamehameha the Great, then paramount chief of the island of Hawai'i. (If Kamehameha had been defeated in this battle, perhaps we would refer to the island group as the O'ahuan Islands rather than the Hawaiian Islands.)

In 1795, the warriors of Kamehameha I, having conquered Maui and Moloka'i on the way from the island of Hawai'i, landed along the southern coast of O'ahu, covering the beaches from Waikīkī to Wai'alae with their war canoes. Meeting the defenders near Punchbowl, the invading armies forced the local warriors up Nu'uanu Valley to the Pali. Kalanikūpule, the defending chief, held the pass with his warriors, allowing women, children, and elders to flee to the Windward side. At this juncture, however, the forces of Kamehameha were hindered in their advance by two cannons Kalanikūpule had installed along the ridge in notches more than 12 feet deep and 30 feet wide. These notches can still be seen along the east side of the upper ridge. Kamehameha therefore sent runners to Waikīkī, directing a small group of warriors to

It is not known when the Nu'uanu Pali Notches were constructed, if they were built in the late 18th century for the sole purpose of serving as cannon positions for the decisive Battle of Nu'uanu, or whether, like similar earthen fortifications elsewhere in the islands, they were designed for more ancient warfare.

proceed up Mānoa Valley and over the sharp Kōnāhuanui summit to remove the gun implacements. Once this was achieved, the Hawaiian warriors thrust forward, pushing the defenders over the precipitous *pali*. According to another report, the O'ahu armies jumped of their own accord, rather than surrender. In 1897, construction of Pali Road unearthed 800 skulls and other bones at the foot of the cliff, believed to be the remains of the defeated O'ahu warriors. After the battle, a young O'ahu chiefess named her firstborn child Kaheananui ("the great heap of corpses") in memory of the hundreds who had died in the 600-foot plunge over the *pali*.

It is not known when the Nu'uanu Pali Notches were constructed, if they were built in the late 1700s for the sole purpose of serving as cannon positions, or whether they were designed for more ancient warfare, like similar earthen fortifications cut into Pauoa and Wa'ahila ridges above Mānoa Valley.

One should not attempt to climb up to the notches, but safely view them from the park below. *(13/116; 14/30; 28/314–315)*

11   *Pōhaku Ka Luahine*

Large boulder with petroglyphs

LOCATION: On the Honolulu side of Moanalua Stream, visible from the jeep trail above Moanalua Valley Park. The stone is near post #10, under a mango tree beside the seventh stone bridge. Allow one hour for the round-trip hike.

A mile or so up Moanalua trail in Kamana Nui Valley (at marker #10), beside the stream and adjacent to one of several turn-of-the-19th-century stone bridges, is a large boulder known as Pōhaku Ka Luahine. The boulder is carved with petroglyphs and is considered sacred.

A number of figures, mostly human, are carved on the surface of the stone. Now well worn by the elements, but still visible, are 22 identifiable units, as well as a 90-dot *kōnane* board (a game similar to checkers). Some of the human images are of the stick-figure type common in many regions of the Pacific and believed to be of an early date. There are no human figures with triangular bodies or distinctly shaped musculature at this site. Some of the clustered petroglyphs suggest family groupings.

One petroglyph on Pōhaku Ka Luahine, the figure of a person whose left arm extends into a wavy line as though cracking a whip, is unique to Kamana Nui Valley. The only stone carving like it in Hawai'i is also in this valley. In another area of the stone appear zoomorphic bird-men, perhaps connected with bird gathering practices or spirit-flight experiences.

An unusual high-relief petroglyph carving, also of bird-men, was found on a small boulder in the valley and has been moved to

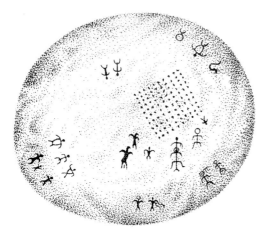

The Pōhaku Ka Luahine, formerly known as the Laupo Stone, in Moanalua Valley, has a 90-point *kōnane* board (right center), numerous human figures, including a family with child (far left), and what appears to be a zoomorphic pair of bird-beings (lower center).

This high-relief carving on a small boulder from Moanalua Valley is now in the Bishop Museum collection. The curvilinear, anthropomorphic forms are stylistically unlike other Hawaiian petroglyphs, but bear a striking resemblance to Rapa Nui (Easter Island) petroglyphs that are connected to rituals involving the sooty tern's annual return to this isolated South Pacific island.

Bishop Museum. The curvilinear zoomorphic forms are back to back in an active squatting position, as if dancing, praying, or making an offering. They are stylistically very unlike any other Hawaiian petroglyphs, but bear a striking similarity to Rapa Nui (Easter Island) carvings that celebrate a bird-man cult on that South Pacific island in honor of the sooty tern's annual migration. For this reason the Moanalua stone is something of a mystery.

Pōhaku Ka Luahine (also written Kapōhakuluahine) means "stone of the old woman," perhaps alluding to a local tale of a small child who cried during the consecration of a *heiau* in lower Moanalua Valley (probably Paliuli or Koaloa Heiau). Because any kind of noise during such a ritual was an offense punishable by death, the child's grandmother, wishing to protect the infant, ran with it up the valley to an area called Kahaukomo, and hid behind this boulder. Warriors searching for the old woman and child could not find them. After a few days the *kapu* of silence ended and the child, now safe from danger, was returned home by its caring grandmother.

Concrete has been used to help support the stone and prevent it from slipping into the stream below. *(16; 20/100–101; 23/10; 28/337–338)*

An 11-mile hike up the back of the valley will take one to the summit of the Ko'olau Range at 1,680 feet and afford one a view over into Ha'ikū Valley on the Windward side. The Stairway to Heaven (a lengthy complex of ladders) is to the right and can be descended to the other side of the *pali.*

Kamana Nui Valley is presently open to the public. Information about the area and a helpful and informative guide booklet are available from Moanalua Gardens Foundation (808-839-5334).

12 *Maunalua and Paikō Lagoon*

Coastal ponds and bay

LOCATION: Paikō Lagoon is at the end of Bay Street, *makai* (seaward) off Kalaniana'ole Highway, adjacent to Kuli'ou'ou Beach Park parking lot. The former Loko Kuapā/Keahupua o Maunalua Fishpond (Koko Marina) can be seen from Koko Marina Shopping Center, Hawai'i Kai Towne Center, and Hawai'i Kai Shopping Center. Maunalua Bay is accessed from the Maunalua Bay Beach Park, *makai* of Kalaniana'ole Highway, and opposite the end of Hawai'i Kai Drive.

It is said that the goddess Hi'iaka, Pele's sister, stopped in this eastern region of O'ahu on her way through Wailupe and Niu (these latter areas both had coastal fishponds that have since been filled in; Wailupe Fishpond and Kupapa Fishpond respectively). In Kuli'ou'ou, Hi'iaka begged some fisher women for part of their catch in order to feed herself and her hungry spirit-companions, but the women gruffly refused the needy travelers. Hi'iaka blasted the inhospitable fisher women with a chant that cursed them and all fisher folk in the area with a cold coastal wind that chills the naked back and legs. The fisher women dropped dead and Hi'iaka's spirit company continued on their journey to find nourishment and a warmer welcome elsewhere.

In 1786, the second known landing in the islands by British ships was made at Maunalua (Two Mountains) Bay. Captains Portlock (for whom an adjacent neighborhood is named) and Dixon came ashore in search of fresh water and were directed to a spring at the mouth of Kuli'ou'ou Valley, perhaps Kānewai (Kuliwai) or Kalauha'eha'e (Lucas Spring), from which they filled casks with the help of local natives. Kuli'ou'ou means "sounding knee," and refers to

From Paikō Lagoon Wildlife Sanctuary, one can look across Maunalua Bay to Koko Head, the volcanic crater that forms Hanauma Bay.

playing the knee drum, a small percussion instrument tied to the knee and played in connection with *hula*. Following the Great Mahele in 1848, when it became possible to buy and sell property, most of the land and water rights in this area were acquired by Manuel De Pico, a Portuguese whaler, for $800. Pico changed his name to Paikō.

Paikō Lagoon does not appear on some maps of the 1880s, but was counted in a 1930s survey of the area as a fishpond. Paikō Lagoon Wildlife Sanctuary was established in 1981 and is a Marine Protected Area serving a variety of uses. The lagoon is fed by Kuli'ou'ou Stream and freshwater springs. The present water level varies according to tidal changes and often exposes saline mudflats. Paikō Lagoon and the adjacent Kuli'ou'ou Beach Park provide a habitat for migratory birds, including the endangered Hawaiian stilt, or *ae'o*. Kuli'ou'ou Beach Park is a small community park with restrooms and access to the shallow reef flats. Surfers reach Tunas and Turtles surf breaks from here.

Kuliwai (Kānewai) Fishpond is a spring-fed pond just inland of Paikō Pond; the two ponds are connected by a *mākāhā* (sluice gate). The smaller (3.3 acres), private pond is jointly owned by the residents of the homes around it. It is sometimes refered to as Kānewai (not the pond-spring mentioned in Mānoa Valley legends) because of a spring of the same name that feeds it. A 1975 fishpond survey lists it as a royal pond but it was apparently constructed in the 20th century. This pond is privately owned and not accessible to the public.

Another nearby, inaccessible pond is Kalauha'eha'e, also known as Lucas Spring. A summer home site of King Kamehameha I

A fish petroglyph on private land near Loko Kuapā/ Keahupua o Maunalua Fishpond (Koko Marina) demonstrates the importance of the fishing resources in the area.

and Queen Ka'ahumanu, the pond flow was damaged in a highway-widening project in the early 1990s that led to condemnation of the property. However, if all goes according to plan, the site may soon be restored and open to small groups of kūpuna, cultural practitioners, scientists, and professional educators.

Loko Kuapā (fishpond wall) or Kuapā Pond was located where the present 523-acre waterway known as Koko Marina is situated. It has two accesses to Maunalua Bay, and extends back toward Haha'ione and Kamilo Nui Valleys. It was dredged, beginning in 1959, and is now a private marina. In former times the pond was known as Keahupua o Maunalua Fishpond and was said to be inhabited by a mo'o called Laukupu. She looked after the fish and responded according to the offerings of the people.

The pond was restored in the early 19th century by Kamehameha I, and later leased to Charles R. Bishop by Princess Kamāmalu. In 1883, the area was inherited by Princess Bernice Pauhi Bishop from the Kamehameha land holdings, and Bishop Estate leased the fishpond to a series of Hawaiian and Chinese konohiki. A 5,000-foot rock wall separated the pond from the bay until the 1930s when it was widened for a roadway. At this time there were eleven recognized fishponds in the East O'ahu area, including: the expansive Maunalua Fishpond, Paikō, Kupapa, Kamoana, Wailupe, Punakou, and five other unnamed fishponds. Maunalua or Kuapā specialized in mullet and was very productive into the 1940s and '50s. There are legends of an underwater tunnel that was said to explain the sudden influx and disappearence of certain kinds of fish at the pond. *(28/270–274; 32)*

Paikō Lagoon Wildlife Sanctuary is managed by the Hawai'i Department of Land and Natural Resources. Additional monitoring of the Maunalua Bay area are organized by Mālama Maunalua, a community-based alliance dedicated to preserving the cultural and ecological heritage of coastal East O'ahu (malamamaunalua.org), and the Maunalua Fishpond Heritage Center (ccramer@maunaluafishpondheritage.org). See also www.maunalua.net.

13 *Pāhua Heiau*

Terraced rock construction

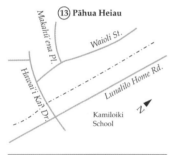

(13) Pāhua Heiau

Makahū'ena Pl.
Waioli St.
Hawai'i Kai Dr.
Lunalilo Home Rd.
Kamiloiki
School

**LOCATION: 7144 Makahū'ena
Place, between Kamilo Iki and
Kamilo Nui Valleys.**

Pāhua Heiau is situated at the end of a ridge, between Kamilo Nui and Kamilo Iki Valleys, where it has a commanding view of the former Loko Kuapā/Keahupua o Maunalua Fishpond (Koko Marina), flanked by Mariner's Ridge and Koko Crater. Kamilo Nui, to the west, is one of the few remaining productive agricultural areas in this region.

The *heiau* is a 68 foot by 40 foot rock terrace with several low dividing walls. Only the eastern portion of the temple has been restored. It would have extended further along the base of the ridge and would have displayed basic wooden architectural features thatched with *pili* grass. White coral pieces may still be seen in the temple foundation, something that usually appears at *heiau* sites, and when radiocarbon dated can help to determine the age of the structure.

This 14th-century temple was most likely dedicated to agricultural production and animal husbandry. Like the now destroyed Hawea Heiau that is at the foot of Mariner's Ridge (the next ridge to the west), Pāhua would have served much of the Maunalua area. It may have also held a function in connection with fishing because of its proximity to Loko Kuapā/Keahupua o Maunalua Fishpond. In the late 19th and early 20th centuries, the Maunalua area was used for cattle ranching and pig farming.

The *heiau* site retains a particularly peaceful feeling, in spite of being surrounded by suburbia. The site was first maintained by the Outdoor Circle, and then by the Office of Hawaiian Affairs. The Outdoor Circle was responsible for initiating partial restoration of the *heiau* in 1985, and the surrounding area has been more recently landscaped with native plants. *(20/65–66; 28/264–265)*

14 *Hanauma Bay*

Natural feature and rock shelter

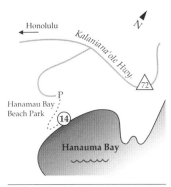

LOCATION: **One half mile east of Hawai'i Kai, off Kalaniana'ole Highway 72.**

PHONE: **(808) 396-4229**

HOURS: **6 a.m. to 6 p.m., daily except Tuesdays**

ADMISSION: **$1 parking; $7 per person; free for children under 13 and for Hawai'i residents with proof of residency.**

Maunalua means "two mountains," and the two mountains are Koko Head, the low, long one, and Koko Crater (see Site 16), the tall, sharp one as seen from Maunalua Bay. An older name for Koko Head is Kawaihoa, meaning "the companion's water." The southeastern side of the Head, an extinct volcanic crater, is broken open to the ocean forming one of the most spectacular bays in the world. *Hana* means "bay," and *uma* means "curved." So, Hanauma translates as "curved bay." However, Hanauma was known as a good landing place for canoes from Moloka'i, and from a lookout above the bay called Mo'okua o Kaneapua one can see Moloka'i, Lana'i, and even west Maui and Haleakalā on a clear day. The curved stem of a canoe is called an *uma*, so this may relate the name of the bay to its function as an active canoe landing.

Hana can also mean "to do," and *uma* can mean "hand-wrestling." Thus, "to do hand-wrestling." This meaning may refer to the Hawaiian legend of two chiefs who engaged in a hand-wrestling match for the love of the beautiful maiden, Keohinani. The winner of the contest was to have Keohinani for his wife. However, the two young chiefs were so equally matched in strength that Keohinani feared they would both die in the struggle of the competition. She prayed to the gods that they would resolve the situation, and this they did by turning her into the wonderfully rounded hills that surround Hanauma Bay so that her two suitors, and everyone who looked upon her, could enjoy her beauty and loveliness. Her father took the shape of a *mo'o*-lizard, curled around as Koko Head beside the water's edge, and formed the protective arms of Hanauma Bay.

Hawaiian fishermen used a rock shelter at Hanauma Bay for temporary protection from the elements. Excavated in 1952, the shelter yielded numerous shells, bones, and fishhooks.

After Kamehameha I took control of O'ahu, his wife Queen Ka'ahumanu visited the bay and was entertained here for a month with *hula* and *uma* competitions. This is also how the bay may have aquired its name. It continued to be an occasional gathering place for royalty and a favorite fishing ground for the later King Kamehameha V.

There is a little-noticed rock shelter at Hanauma Bay that was used by Hawaiian fishermen for temporary protection from the elements. When it was excavated in 1952, archaeologists uncovered numerous shells, bones of dogs and pigs, a shark's tooth, a carved bone, shell beads, a bone pick, cooking stones, and 22 fishhooks. The site is to the left, at the bottom of the drive. It is fenced, overgrown, and dates back several hundred years. *(13/115; 28/267; 29/29, 44)*

For most of the last century, Hanauma Bay has been a favorite local beach and picnic area. When the tourist industry discovered the bay, it became a popular attraction and overuse occurred that put the area in danger. Since then Hanauma Bay Nature Preserve, the first Marine Life Conservation District in the State of Hawai'i, has been established. This provides oversight and a certain amount of protection for the bay.

15 Koko Head Petroglyphs

Rock carvings on raised floor of sea cave

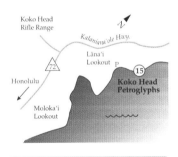

LOCATION: Between Lāna'i Lookout and the Japanese fishermen shrine, below Kalaniana'ole Highway. There is a pull-off area large enough for three or four cars, and from there you can step over the guard rail and climb down the thirty-foot cliff to the shelf below. This trek is not recommended for everyone, as it requires climbing up and down steep, sometimes slippery rocks.

First recorded in 1899, these petroglyphs originally included some 37 figures, mostly human, cut into the rough, slanting basalt floor of an exposed sea cave at water's edge. Today only a few figures remain, the rest having been destroyed by weather and vandalism (an entire section of rock has been deliberately cut away).

The figures that remain are cut 1/16 to 3/4 of an inch deep into the rock and are three different sizes: 6, 9, and 15 inches in length. The human figures all point their arms downwards. (Of the original petroglyphs, the one human figure depicted with arms raised was vandalized prior to 1904.) A sail, a dog, and surfer on his board were some of the other themes that appeared among the carvings.

At high tide, the surf washes the mouth of the cave. If you visit at this time, take care at the water's edge, for this area is known for its rough surf, strong currents, and dangerous undertow. *(20/67–68; 28/265–266; 29/32–33)*

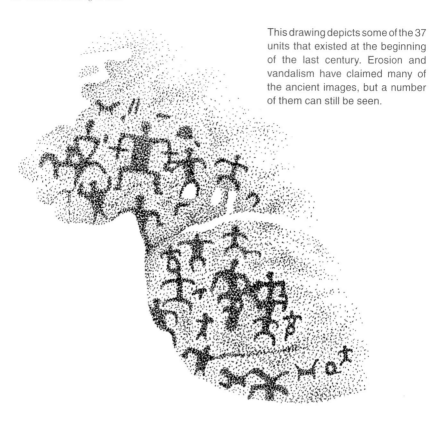

This drawing depicts some of the 37 units that existed at the beginning of the last century. Erosion and vandalism have claimed many of the ancient images, but a number of them can still be seen.

Carved on an uplifted and slanted slab of basalt within a sea cave, the Koko Head Petroglyphs were much more extensive in the early 20th century when the first rubbings and drawings were made from them.

Koko Head Petroglyphs are tucked away, just out of sight, in a gash in the coastal face.

16 *Kohelepelepe*

Extinct volcanic crater

LOCATION: **Off Kealahou Street in the Queen's Gate area. The crater can easily be seen looking west from Kalaniana'ole Highway near Hawai'i Kai Golf Course.**

Kohelepelepe is the open eastern side of Koko Crater. The site received its name, which means "traveling vagina," from a clever act of the goddess Kapo who exposed her genitalia in order to save her sister Pele from the clutches of the pursuing pig god, Kamapua'a. The ruse apparently worked, for Pele got away, and Kapo, one of Pele's sisters, left a *pali pōhaku* (rocky cliff) resembling her private part as a monument to her deed.

Another Hawaiian tale tells of a local *ali'i* maiden who had been raised away from home, as was often the custom. Returning to the area and finding her parents absent, she innocently ate some of their sugarcane growing in a nearby field. Not knowing that her father, the chief, had asked the shark god to protect his sugar crop from thieves, the girl went for a swim and was mauled by a shark. While still badly bleeding, she wandered around the area of Koko Crater and Koko Head. *Koko* is Hawaiian for "blood."

Inside the crater is Koko Crater Botanical Park, maintained by the City and County of Honolulu. A walk around the inside of the arid crater to see the Hawaiian, African, and cactus gardens takes about an hour and is pleasant on a cool day. *(26/115; 28/267; 29/43–44)*

17   *Kapaliokamoa* (Pele's Chair)

Large lava rock formation

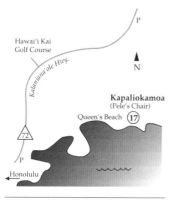

LOCATION: Off Kalaniana'ole Highway, at the end of the ridge above Queen's Beach. It is easily viewed from the highway, between Hawai'i Kai Golf Club and Makapu'u Lookout, and can be approached on foot from the Makapu'u Lighthouse car park.

This lava rock formation at the end of a ridge in the Ka Iwi (The Bones) coastal region was called Kapaliokamoa (The Cliff of the Chicken) by Hawaiians. This is presumably because of its perching, bird-like appearance; from a certain perspective it looks like a squatting chicken. It was also refered to as Queen's Chair, perhaps because it presides over nearby Queen's Beach. However, it is mostly known today as Pele's Chair, in reference to the volcano goddess who formed the island by means of her volcanic activity. This spot is said to be one of the places from which the volcano goddess left O'ahu to continue her work on other islands to the east. Her O'ahu tasks completed, she vacated her chair at the water's edge and headed for Moloka'i and Lāna'i; they can both be seen from here on a clear day. (The island's geologic formation was in fact finished here at its southeastern-most end, and Moloka'i and Lāna'i were formed after O'ahu.) Seen from the Hawai'i Kai Golf Club and on the road to Makapu'u, the lava outcrop looks very much like a giant chair or throne. However, up close it loses this appearance.

Legend tells of Hi'iaka, Pele's sister, coming through this area and encouraging Makapu'u and Malei, two female *kupua* (supernatural, shapechanging beings), to cultivate sweet potatoes on the coastal plain in order to quell their hunger. Makapu'u means "hill beginning" or "bulging eye," and this goddess was said to have many eyes. There was a stone near the point, no longer there, in the shape of her unusual form. Malei also had a *pōhaku* (stone) figure and was said to attract fish to the area waters. She stood on the cliff above the present lighthouse. Bishop Museum requested the stone to be added to its collection back in the early 20th century, but the white rock image disappeared shortly thereafter.

In his travels around O'ahu in 1826, Levi Chamberlain, a visiting New England missionary, noted in his diary that companions of his attempted unsuccessfully to knock down a "pagan image" in the area of Makapu'u. Judging from his description, it could very well have been the *pōhaku* figure of Makapu'u or Malei. It is not likely that it was Kapaliokamoa (Pele's Chair) because of this stone's very large size.

Several *pōhaku* of significance were washed out to sea in 1946 when a major tidal wave swept across this side of the island below Pele's Chair. Another stone reported in the area was called "Pele's Canoe," a gouged boulder imprinted with a grooved trough as though a canoe hull had been impressed into the solid rock, the effect of cooling lava. This was said to be a mark from Pele's own canoe, and appears to be another story that suggests the Hawaiians were aware of the departure of Pele's volcanic activity from this end of O'ahu. The stone was located below Kapaliokamoa on the other side of Kaho'ohaihai Inlet.

In 1998, the State of Hawai'i sought to condemn the privately owned coastland where Kapaliokamoa is located, and in 2001, it agreed to pay $12.8 million to Kamehameha Schools in order to secure its future and prevent any further development of the area. Ka Iwi Coast, from Hanauma Bay to Makapu'u, is being considered for a State Park. *(24/X-24–25; 28/258–260; 29/30)*

II. Windward Side

A Waimānalo *ko'a* (fishing shrine) just off-shore at Makapu'u was destroyed by a tidal wave in 1946. Having served the needs of ancient fishermen who lived at Kaupō (also called Ko'onāpou) village, the *ko'a* honored the fish goddess Malei, who provided an abundance of *moi* (threadfish) and *uhu* (parrot fish) to the faithful. The *ko'a*, an uneven stone pile measuring 15 feet by 25 feet and rising about 10 feet above the surface of the water at low tide, may have been related to the nearby fishing shrine, Pōhaku Pa'akikī (Site 18), which was damaged by the same tidal wave *(18/25–255)*. (Bishop Museum Archives, 1930)

The Windward side of O'ahu is so named because of the steady and reliable trade winds that bless its shores, valleys, and mountains with a good deal of wet and windy weather. The region stretches from Waimānalo in the southeast to Kualoa in the north, and is overseen by the towering, fortress-like cliffs of the Ko'olau mountain range.

Windward O'ahu includes the populated areas of Kailua and Kāne'ohe, but unlike the Honolulu region of East O'ahu, it still retains a good number of archaeological sites, especially *heiau*. Some of these temple ruins are on the Register of Historic Places: Leleahina in He'eia, believed to be the burial place of Keli'ikanaka'ole and his wife Kopaea; Kawa'ewa'e in Kāne'ohe, built by Chief 'Olopana in the 12th century, but also attributed to Menehune; and Pōhakunui, Olomana, and Pueo Heiau in Waimānalo. The less-known Ka'alaea Valley Heiau is

Mānana Island can easily be seen from Pāhonu Pond, a former turtle pond (Site 19).

thought by some to have been an agricultural *heiau*, largely because of its location in the lush and fertile valley whose name means "red earth." Unfortunately, most of these *heiau* have not been fully excavated or are not readily accessible to the public. However, the easy-to-find Ulupō Heiau State Monument (Site 20) is a wonderful exception. This temple overlooks Kawai Nui Marsh and dates back to AD 400, according to radiocarbon dating. Just across the marsh is Pahukini Heiau, which does require permission to access. Nearby, at Bellows Beach, excavations have uncovered the earliest cultural deposits in Hawai'i, dated at AD 323.

This area of the island is probably the best for spotting the remains of ancient fishponds, and one can even find a former turtle pond (Site 19). Although many ponds are difficult to get close to, it is possible to glimpse some of the old ponds while driving along coastal roads; He'eia Fishpond (Site 26) and Kahalu'u Fishpond (Site 27) are good examples.

An important site on the Windward coast is Mōkapu ("sacred district"). It is here that Hawaiian lore tells of the first man and woman being created. Unfortunately, this area is not easily accessible because it is on an active U.S. military base. However, Nu'upia Ponds (Site 24) can be seen from outside the restricted area.

One of the most important accessible sites on the Windward side, in fact on the entire island, is Kualoa (Site 29). This was a *pu'uhonua*, a place of refuge for those who had broken *kapu* or were fleeing their enemies in times of war. It was also the residence of chiefs and a place where *ali'i* children were educated. According to oral tradition, victims to be offered as sacrifice at area *heiau* were drowned here and left floating like the seaweed of Kawahine (*ka limu o Kawahine*). Kualoa was the seat of the priesthood of Lono, the god of agriculture, and the last stop of the Makahiki procession on its journey around O'ahu. Kualoa was also a favorite canoe landing in the old days and it was here in 1987 that the *Hōkūle'a*, an ancient-style double-hulled sailing canoe returned from a two-year pan-Pacific voyage that proved non-instrument navigation was possible throughout Polynesia.

Ha'ikū Valley, Luluku agricultural terraces, and Kukui o Kāne Heiau are some other important Windward sites. See Hālawa-Luluku Interpretive Development Area (Site 44), listed in the Central O'ahu section of this book, for these other Ko'olau Poko sites.

Ko'olau Poko is the Hawaiian name for this Windward part of O'ahu. It means the "short windward side."

Map of Windward Side

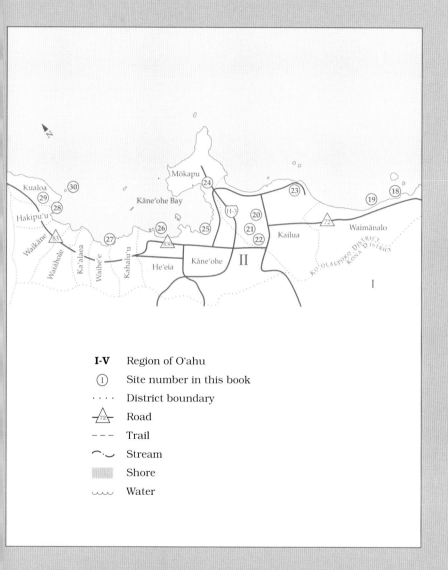

I-V	Region of Oʻahu
①	Site number in this book
· · · ·	District boundary
△72	Road
- - -	Trail
⌒⌣	Stream
▓	Shore
∿∿	Water

18   *Pōhaku Pa'akikī*

Large stone on beach

LOCATION: On the shoreline between the Makai Research Pier and Sea Life Park, opposite the Oceanic Institute.

This large stone is washed by waves at low tide and covered by water at high tide. Pa'akikī measures 93 inches in length, 79 inches in width, and is 26 inches thick. At one time another stone supported the Pa'akikī stone so that it was positioned like a tabletop.

Pōhaku Pa'akikī was sacred to local sweet potato farmers who offered 'awa (a root that acts as a natural narcotic) daily to Kamohoali'i, their shark god. Legend holds that a fisherman, trying to provoke the farmers, caught sharks and threw their severed tails into the water by this *pōhaku.* Naturally, this annoyed Kamohoali'i, who caught the fisherman in the water one day and began to devour him, beginning with his feet. The shark god stopped at the fisherman's buttocks because of the smell of excrement, and the spirit of Kamohoali'i revealed to one of the farmers his pledge to never again eat human flesh or allow other sharks to harm anyone between Makapu'u and Waimānalo. For many years thereafter, no shark-related injuries were reported in this area. Perhaps, too, it is no coincidence that Pōhaku Pa'akikī is near Kalaeki'ona ("dung-heap") Point.

It is here at Makapu'u that the legendary volcano goddess Pele directed the fish goddess Mālei to watch over the eastern shores of O'ahu. Perhaps this is why these waters are so plentiful with fish. The old Hawaiian village of Kaupō, meaning "night landing," was formerly where Sea Life Park and the Oceanic Institute are today.

Native Hawaiians occupied the small coastal park on the *makai* side of the road in a housing protest between 1993 and 1994. A group called the Children of Kū built a rock wall enclosure, a modern *heiau*, to the four traditional gods: Kū, Lono, Kāne, and Kanaloa which can still be seen today. *(28/252)*

Just off shore is Mānana Island, better known as Rabbit Island, and Moku Hope, called Shark Rock. Two other exposed rocks here are Kaohi'ipu and Kahalaoia. (See Site 19.)

Native Hawaiian group, Children of Kū, built this rock wall enclosure, a modern *heiau*, to the four traditional gods: Kū, Lono, Kāne, and Kanaloa.

19   Pāhonu Pond

Coastal stone wall enclosure

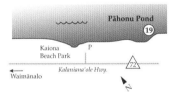

LOCATION: In the water just south of Kaiona Beach Park (adjacent to the former "Magnum P.I." television location). You can wade up to this site or just view it from Kaiona Beach Park.

Restored as a breakwater, this stone rampart surrounded a turtle pond for the *aliʻi* of the district. Turtle meat was forbidden to all but the chiefs under penalty of death, but local fishermen were required to keep the pond supplied with the delicacy. Partially submerged at high tide, the wall originally enclosed an area about 500 feet by 60 feet and ran up to Kaiona Beach Park, from which it is accessible.

Mānana Island, also known as Rabbit Island, is a tuff cone rising above the ocean's surface beyond Pāhonu Pond. The island was the site of two *koʻa* (fishing shrines) as well as ancient burials. It is a bird sanctuary and may be visited only by special arrangement from the State of Hawaiʻi. *(26/174; 28/249)*

20 *Ulupō Heiau*

Extensive stone platform

LOCATION: On the Kāne'ohe side of Kailua Road, at the end of Manu 'Ō'o Road, behind the YMCA.

Measuring 140 feet by 180 feet across, and 30 feet in height, this ancient *heiau* foundation is impressive in size and commands a sweeping view of Kawainui Marsh, a former fishpond. It is the largest surviving platform *heiau* on O'ahu, but not the largest in overall length (see Site 35). Because of its location adjacent to fertile farmland, Ulupō may have been an agricultural *heiau*. However, because of its size and oral tradition it may have also been used to assert political power by the warrior chief Kūali'i in the 1600s, and by Kākuhihewa and possibly Kahekili of Maui in the 1700s. The *heiau* was abandoned by 1795 when Kamehameha the Great conquered O'ahu.

Ulupō means "night inspiration" and the *heiau* is said to have been built in one night by Menehune who passed the rocks, which average 12 to 18 inches in diameter, from hand to hand over a great distance. A trail at the site, refered to as the "Menehune Pathway," leads down to a spring at the northwest corner of the *heiau*. The spring feeds two small pools, each about 3 feet in diameter. It is said that pigs brought to the *heiau* as offerings were washed in the springs before sacrifice.

The path across the center of the platform leads to what is said to be a former *hale* site. Occasionally, small offerings are left near the plaque that dedicates this historic site. The site is on Hawai'i State Park Reserve land and is cared for by the Kailua Hawaiian Civic Club and Ka Pā Kui-a-Holo. They offer service/learning projects, and together with 'Ahahui Mālama I Ka Lōkahi, they have restored the spring-fed *lo'i kalo* (taro patches) at the base of the *heiau. (13/74–75, 115; 20/186–188; 26/215; 28/232–234)*

Offerings are occasionally left beside the plaque that dedicates this historic site.

21   *Nā Pōhaku o Hauwahine*

Rock outcrop

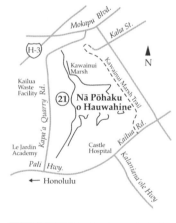

**LOCATION: On right side of
Kapa'a Quarry Road, at the Y-
intersection before the Kapa'a
Landfill Transfer Station. One
mile from Kalaniana'ole Highway
intersection.**

Every body of water in Hawai'i had a spirit being, a lizard- or mermaid/merman-like creature, which was its keeper. Kawai Nui ("the big waters") was an extensive 400-acre, inland fishpond at one time and Hauwahine was its *mo'o* or water spirit. Nā Pōhaku o Hauwahine is an outcrop of large sacred boulders at the western edge of Kawai Nui Marsh, named for the guardian of the pond. The freshwater pond belonged to the *ali'i* and was well known locally for the finest fat mullet and easy to catch *'awa* fish.

When the goddess Hi'iaka, Pele's younger sister, was traveling through the Windward area with her companion, Wahineoma'o, the latter commented on two beautiful women sitting on a rock by the pond. Hi'iaka replied: "Those are not real women, but lizards [*mo'o*]." Wahineoma'o's disbelief prompted Hi'iaka to say that if she chanted and they disappeared then they must be *mo'o*. She proceeded to chant:

> Kailua is like hair tousled by the Malanai
> wind
> The leaves of the *uki* are flattened down
> You are startled as though by the voice of
> a bird

You think they are human
But they are not
That is Hauwahine and her companion
The supernatural women of Kailua.

When the beautiful figures beside the pond heard Hi'iaka, they glanced at each other and vanished. Hi'iaka explained to Wahineoma'o that Hauwahine belonged to Kawai Nui as its guardian and the other being belonged to the *hala* grove on the level place near Ka'elepulu Stream. When the *mo'o* are present the *hala* leaves, *uki* grass, and bulrushes turn a yellowish hue. It is also said that when Hi'iaka saw Hauwahine bathing, the lizard's "bird flew up and obscured the sun." This, according to some historians, may indicate the occurrence of a solar eclipse.

The fishpond and *lo'i kalo* (taro paddies) had been abandoned by the early 20th century and became an 850-acre wetland, the largest in the islands. Nā Pōhaku o Hauwahine, the rock outcropping, offers panoramic views into the *piko*, or navel, of the marsh. The designated 12-acre State Park around the *pōhaku* is now cared for by 'Āhahui Mālama I Ka Lōkahi, a non-profit conservation group. Service projects are held the third Saturday of each month and are the best way to experience the site. *(28/230–231)*

CONTACT: **'Āhahui Mālama I Ka Lōkahi, P.O. Box 751, Honolulu, HI 96808**

PHONE: **(808) 263-8008**

WEBSITE: **www.ahahui.net**

Na Pōhaku o Hauwahine presents a panoramic view into the *piko*, or navel, of the marsh and 12-acre State Park.

22   *Pahukini Heiau*

Walled stone structure

Earlier called Makini and Mo'okini, this *heiau* is presently known as Pahukini, meaning "many drums." Though little is known concerning the origins or uses of the *heiau*, a plaque at the site says it was built by Chief 'Olopana about AD 1100. Burials are known to have occurred within the platform area.

One of the largest religious sites on the Windward side, measuring about 120 feet by 180 feet, Pahukini Heiau is a rectangular enclosure of stacked rock walls once measuring 6 feet in height. A smaller enclosure and opening along the north wall are believed to be later additions. Paving stones used for the *heiau* floor are piled in small mounds within the walls. The *heiau* was originally positioned on flatter ground, however, slope erosion, quarrying, and the city landfill have greatly impacted the temple, nearly collaps-

LOCATION: Inside the Kapa'a City Landfill, off Quarry Road, above Kawai Nui Swamp Regional Park, Kailua. Ask the guard at the entrance gate for directions.

ing one of its sides. Quarrying in the 1950s left the *heiau* precariously positioned on a 200-foot cliff. Though at one time it must have commanded a breathtaking view of the hills, valleys, and ocean, its vista of the sea is today greatly diminished by the build-up of the dump, and it now has the busy H-3 Interstate Highway and the starkly quarried mountains as its neighbors.

The *heiau* is enclosed within a locked, chain link fence inside the Kapaʻa City Landfill. However, the site can be accessed with permission. *(20/182–183; 26/174; 28/228)*

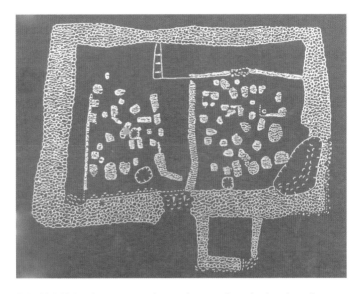

Pahukini Heiau is a rectangular enclosure of stacked rock walls once standing 6 feet in height and measuring about 120 feet wide by 180 feet long. A smaller enclosure and opening along the north wall are believed to be later additions. The site is both a state and national Registered Historic Place.

23 *Kānepolu*

Outcrop of large stones on promontory

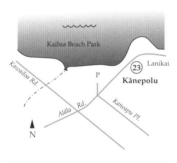

LOCATION: At the top of Alāla Point, visible from Alāla Road and the beach between Kailua and Lanikai.

This basalt rock formation on the highest spot of Alāla ("awakening") Point is now partially obscured by a house that was built directly over the site. The front end of the house actually encloses the upper portion of the rock, which has been fashioned into living room furniture.

Kānepolu was a legendary man who was born, grew up, and died on the same day. He was said to have been summoned by King Kamehameha III, who was staying in a cave below Alāla Point. Upon his arrival, Kānepolu slipped on a large coral rock, killing himself and leaving an impression of his leg in the rock. The upright stones in back of the house are guards waiting for Kānepolu.

This *pōhaku* is also believed to have been a fishing shrine (*koʻa*) that helped fishermen out at sea get their bearings and locate good fishing grounds. It may have been a fish god as well.

Tours of the house have been announced in the past in the local paper. However, this is a private residence and should not be trespassed, but viewed from Kailua Beach below. *(28/238)*

This *pōhaku*, possibly part of a fishing shrine (*koʻa*), is said to be one of the guards waiting for Kānepolu.

24 Nu'upia Ponds

Eight enclosed ponds

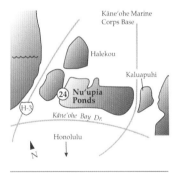

LOCATION: At the end of H-3 Interstate Highway and Kāne'ohe Bay Drive, bordering the Kāne'ohe Marine Corps Air Station on Mōkapu Peninsula. This site is best viewed from inside the Marine base (by arrangement) or from the pedestrian walkway where Kāne'ohe Bay Drive meets H-3.

According to Hawaiian creation chants, it is on Mōkapu Peninsula where the first man was co-created by Kāne, Kaneloa, Kū, and Lono out of the red soil that mingles with very dark bluish-black earth. Kāne drew an image with head, trunk, and limbs in the soil—in the likeness of the gods. Then, all four gods called the image to life and brought the first man to live at Halekou. The first man noticed his shadow followed him everywhere, and when he woke up one day to find a pretty women beside him he assumed the gods made him a wife from his shadow. He there-fore called her Keakahulilani ("the shadow made of heaven"). Mōkapu means "sacred district," and it is for this reason that Kamehameha I met with his high chiefs in council here. Also, a large number of Hawaiian sand burial sites have been excavated in this area, another reason why it might be considered a "sacred district."

A legend tells of a fisher-boy named Puniakai'a ("devoted to fish") who regularly caught and tamed *uhu* (parrot fish) in this area. One of the fish he caught was called Uhumāka'ika'i, the "parent of all fish," and it made its home at Nu'upia Fishpond. The boy and the fish became faithful companions. Puniakai'a's father and mother were Nu'upia and Halekou, and they were of the royal blood of Ko'olau Loa and Ko'olau Poko. They are also the names of two fishponds at Mōkapu.

In ancient times, three ponds separated Mōkapu Peninsula from the rest of Kāne'ohe: Nu'upia, Halekou, and Kaluapuhi Fishponds. They have been somewhat altered in shape and number, but still reveal original dividing walls in places. There are now eight ponds: Nu'upia 'Ekahi, 48 acres; Nu'upia 'Elua, 19 acres; Nu'upia 'Ekolu, 95 acres; Nu'upia 'Eha, 5.7 acres; Halekou, 32 acres; Heleloa, 1.15 acres; Kaluapuhi, 17 acres; and Pa'akai, 26 acres. Kaluapuhi Pond is where the *mo'o* of the ponds is said to live. These ponds are of the *loko kuapā* type, meaning they are built with a wall on a reef. Halekou Pond is enclosed by a 5-foot wide double wall that has dirt fill between the walls. Kapoho is a more recently formed pond, not usually counted with the others, adjoining Kailua Bay and is the site of a former salt works. Ancient Hawaiians collected salt deposits here in leveled, shallow "pans" as the seawater evaporated.

The original ponds are dated to between AD 1300–1600 and became neglected by the mid-1800s. Chinese imigrants leased the ponds to raise *'ama'ama* (mullet) and *awa* (milkfish) for sale in town, and they eventually subdivided the ponds. Today the ponds are collectively a part of the 482-acre Nu'upia Ponds Wildlife Management Area within the Kāne'ohe Marine Corps Air Station. The pond area serves as a habitat for the endangered *kukuluae'o*, a native Hawaiian black-necked stilt. The entire peninsula, including the ponds, is part of an active air base for the United States Marine Corps. Permission is required to access the site. *(13/111; 20/184; 26/153–154; 28/213–217)*

25 *Waikalua Loko Fishpond*

Small, partially walled pond

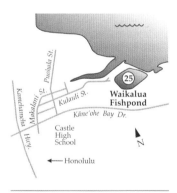

Waikalua Loko is an 11-acre fishpond, situated between the waterways of Kāneʻohe Stream and Kawa Stream. It has a 1,400-foot long *kuapā* (wall) of basalt rock, 3 to 4 feet high and 5 feet wide, with three *mākāhā* (sluice gates) connecting it to Kāneʻohe Bay. The present *mākāhā* were renovated in 1930 using concrete and iron grates to control the tidal flow of water and the entry and exit of fish. Historic records can only trace Waikalua Loko back about 150 years, but analysis of pond walls and sediment floor should determine a more precise age of the pond. The fishpond is thought to be between 350 and 600 years old. Waikalua means "water of the pit" or "water of the fighter," and it also designates the name of the land division around the pond.

The pond is owned by the Bayview Golf Course and cared for by Waikalua Loko Fishpond Preservation Society since 1995. However, there are efforts by the American Pacific Foundation, founded in 1993, to buy the fee-simple property. The non-profit Society and Foundation sponsor educational programs and invite volunteers to help clean up, restore, maintain, and preserve the fishpond. *(25/222; 28/210; 32)*

Waikalua means "water of the pit" or "water of the fighter," and the pond is thought to be between 350 and 600 years old.

CONTACT: **Waikalua Loko Fishpond Preservation Society,
P.O. Box 1917, Kailua, HI 96734**
PHONE: **(808) 262-3261**
WEBSITE: **www.waikaluafishpond.org**

26 He'eia Fishpond

Coastal pond enclosure

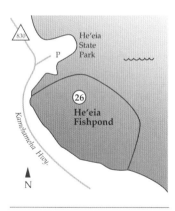

LOCATION (FOR BEST VIEW):
Adjacent to He'eia State Park and
Ke'alohi Point, off Kamehameha
Highway, north of Kāne'ohe.

This 88-acre brackish-water pond is one of the two dozen remaining Hawaiian fishponds in partial use today. Its walls are made of lava with coral fill, and measure more than 12 feet in width and 4 feet in height. There were originally four watchtowers from which pond keepers observed the movement of fish, and six sluice gates, three on the ocean side to allow salt water in and three on the stream side to allow fresh water in. This typical *loko kuapā* had a 5,000-foot long enclosing seawall.

According to legend, a *mo'o* known as Meheanu guarded the fishpond, alternately taking the shape of a frog, lizard, or eel. This *kupua* (shape-changing spirit) was known to be present when the *hau* trees were yellow, but when the leaves were green she dwelt elsewhere in her eel form. Fishermen say she can occasionally be seen in the pond as a beautiful female figure.

An ancient prophecy of victory was fulfilled at this fishpond when, during a battle against a Leeward army, a tidal wave washed (*he'e 'ia*) the local warriors out to sea and then brought them back again to defeat invaders.

Yet another story tells of an *ali'i* who was so jealous of his younger brother that he challenged him to a *he'e nalu*, or surfing competition, and staked all of his property as well as his life on the match. However, it was the older brother who was caught by a swarm of *he'e* (octopus), and killed.

Some say there is no clear tradition of He'eia Fishpond being controlled by royalty before Kamehameha the Great, as were most ponds. This has led to speculation that the fishpond was a truly communal pond, used by all the people of the locale, and not reserved solely for *ali'i*. However, when Kamehameha conquered O'ahu, he took He'eia Fishpond and its lands for himself. Later the pond passed to Princess Bernice Pauahi Bishop and the Bishop Estate.

The pond is best seen from He'eia State Park. Kalae'ula'ula Heiau, now destroyed, was located on Ke'alohi ("the shining") Point within the park boundaries and was once called Kalae'ula-'ula in ancient times, meaning "the red peninsula." The fishpond presently belongs to Kamehameha Schools and is leased to the non-profit organization, Paepae o He'eia. Paepae o He'eia provides eco-cultural activities at the fishpond and has worked together with such organizations as the Oceanic Institute and the National Marine Fisheries Service to revitalize *moi* fish cultivation using ancient Hawaiian methods. Goals include restoring damaged seawalls and bringing the pond back to healthy production levels. Some 2,500 private, public, and charter school students visit the site annually. *(12/32–49; 14/31; 20/173; 28/198–199; 32)*

27 *Kahalu'u Fishpond*

Pond enclosure

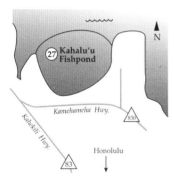

830

**LOCATION: Near the corner
of Kamehameha Highway
and Laenani Drive east of the
intersection of Kamehameha
and Kahekili highways.**

Kahalu'u Pond, which was formerly known as Kahonua Fishpond, has a 1,200-foot long enclosing wall nicely planted with coconut palms. Kahalu'u means "the diving place" or "the dripping trough" and Kahonua means "the earth." At one time the pond had two outlets and one watchtower. The pond lies within a natural cove between Waihe'e Stream in the region of Kahalu'u and Point Wailau on Kāne'ohe Bay.

Hālauakai'amoana Heiau once stood adjacent to the fishpond, but it was destroyed in the early part of the 20th century to make way for a Libby Company pineapple cannery. The cannery's subsequent failure is attributed by local Hawaiians to the desecration of the ancient temple. It is likely that the *heiau* was associated with the fishpond for purposes of propagation and increase of the food supply.

Kahalu'u Fishpond is private property and the site of Aloha Ke Akua Chapel (world-aloha.com; worldofaloha@hawaii.rr.com) where wedding services, *lū'au,* and other events may be arranged. Otherwise the pond is not easily viewed except from offshore and from the air. *(20/170; 26/66; 28/193; 32)*

28   *Mōli'i and 'Āpua Fishponds*

Two pond enclosures

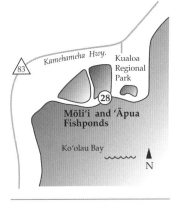

Mōli'i and 'Āpua Fishponds

Ko'olau Bay

N

LOCATION: **On Ko'olau Bay, alongside Kualoa Regional Park off Kamehameha Highway.**

Mōli'i Fishpond was originally formed by enclosing part of Ko'olau Bay with a rockwall that was reinforced over time by shifting sands and beach build-up. The pond is divided into two sections, and originally had five *mākāhā* (sluice gates) connecting it to the bay, only three of which are still operational. Menehune are credited with constructing the pond in one night.

Mōli'i Fishpond is one of the few early royal fishponds that has remained consistantly operational and commercially successful up to the present day. It was bought from Kamehameha III in 1850 by Dr. G. P. Judd, together with 622 acres of land, Mokoli'i Island, and the area's fishing rights. Privately owned by descendants of the family, the pond is now part of a 4,000-acre estate known as Kualoa Ranch (see Site 29).

Mōli'i is a *loko kuapā* estimated to be between 600 and 960 years old and is situated in the *ahupua'a* of Hakipu'u. Its walls are about 11 feet wide, a little more than 5 feet high, and approximately 4,500 feet long. The pond covers 124 acres and ranges in depth from 4 to 30 feet. Currently, 'ama'ama (mullet), moi (threadfish), and awa (milkfish) are raised in the pond and sold locally. In a good three-month season, the pond produces between 7,000 and 10,000 pounds of mullet.

ʻĀpua Pond sits to the east of Mōliʻi Fishpond, and means "fish basket." It is located at the end of the drive that leads into Kualoa Regional Park and can be easily viewed. Along with its neighboring pond Mōliʻi, it is said to be built in pre-recorded times by Menehune. ʻĀpua (also called Pahalona) Pond is often confused with the nearby, no longer existant, Koholālele Pond, but Koholālele was more inland and often described as a long ditch filled with brackish water. Little is known about ʻĀpua, which is often described only as the small pond east of Mōliʻi Fishpond. It is overgrown with brush along its shores and is enclosed by a modern, low, rock wall. The pond apparently fell into disuse towards the end of the 19th and the beginning of the 20th century.

Arrangements can be made to see Mōliʻi Fishpond through the Kualoa Ranch Educational Program. Alternatively, the pond is visible from Kamehamea Highway and by entering Kualoa Regional Park and walking along the beach to an opening in the brush. However, this is a private pond and should not be trespassed. *(20/168; 27; 28/184–185; 32)*

29   *Ahupua'a o Kualoa*

Coastal area

**LOCATION: On both sides of
Kamehameha Highway; Kualoa
Regional Park (*makai*) and
Kualoa Ranch (*mauka*).**

Kualoa means "long back," and refers to the
mountain ridge here as the strength of the
island. Kualoa was a *pu'uhonua* much like
Pu'uhonua o Hōnaunau on the island of Hawai'i,
and was therefore a very sacred area to ancient
Hawaiians, possessing great *mana*. As a place of
refuge, it served those who had broken *kapu* or
were fleeing their enemies in times of war. It was
also the residence of chiefs and a place where
ali'i children were educated. According to oral
tradition, victims to be offered as sacrifice at the
regional *heiau* were drowned here and left floating like the seaweed of Kawahine (*ka limu o
Kawahine*). Kualoa was the seat of the priesthood of Lono, a god of agriculture, and the
beginning and end of the Makahiki procession
that journeyed around the island. Kualoa was
also a favorite canoe landing in the old days and as a sign of
respect for the area's sanctity, Kamehameha the Great lowered
his canoe sails as he passed by the district. In 1987, *Hōkūle'a*, an
ancient-style, double-hulled sailing canoe returned here from a
two-year pan-Pacific voyage that proved non-instrument navigation was possible.

In 1850, Kamehameha III sold Kualoa for $1,300. The land was cultivated in sugar until a milling accident convinced Hawaiian workers that such activities at this sacred place were not right. The remains of the old sugar mill can still be seen beside the highway.

The highest peak on the ridge above Kualoa is known as Puʻu Kānehoalani, named for the father of Pele, a god who "ruled the heavens." The name literally means "Kāne's heavenly companion." Some of the peaks are said to be a woman and her two daughters who were turned to stone at dawn in punishment for not catching beach crabs fast enough during the night. Lower along the cliff face are hollows reputedly made by Kamapuaʻa, the pig god, when he was fleeing from Pele. However, it is also claimed that the mountain was "pierced by Kūʻīlioloa," a legendary *kupua* who appeared as a dog. It is here too that the sacred cave, Pohukaina, was said to be the final resting place of over 150 generations of *aliʻi*. Above Mōliʻi Fishpond, on the *pali* just outside the district of Kualoa, is the Nānāhoa Stone. Described in some legends as a phallic rock, other stories say it is a young boy who was turned into stone after wandering too far from home and staring at a beautiful naked maiden in the water below. Still another legend speaks of Nānāhoa as a thief who was turned to stone on the ridge when he tried to rob Pele.

Kahahana, the ruling chief of Oʻahu in the 1770s, almost gave the Kualoa region to his uncle Kahekili of Maui as a gift for rearing him, but the *kahuna* Kaʻōpulupulu warned Kahahana that if he surrendered the area, he would be giving all of his authority over Oʻahu to the Maui chief. The advice of Kaʻōpulupulu thus temporarily prevented a dramatic shift in power. Kahekili eventually convinced Kahahana to kill the powerful *kahuna*, which then gave the Maui chief good reason to attack and conquer O'ahu.

In ancient times, no less than four *heiau* were in the vicinity. Today, archaeologists can point to the partial remains of the rock platforms of two significant *heiau*: Puakea and Kukuianiani. Both stand on private land not far from the beach park.

In 1850, Kamehameha III sold 622-acres of Kualoa, Mōli'i Fishpond, and the island of Mokoli'i, including all the adjoining fishing grounds, to Dr. Gerrit Judd for $1,300. The land was cultivated in sugar until it was realized the soil was too poor and production was discontinued in 1871. The death of Judd's grandson in a milling accident convinced Hawaiian workers that such activities at this sacred place were not right and they left their jobs. The remains of the old sugar mill can still be seen beside the highway. More land was eventually aquired and a successful cattle ranch was developed. In 1927, with 4,000 acres, the operation became known as Kualoa Ranch. During WWII the military made use of the property, building mountainside bunkers and an airstrip that crossed the highway. Since then Kualoa Ranch has adapted to a tourist economy with diversified activities from horseback riding, cattle ranching, and weddings, to all-terrain vehicle rides, movie locations, and educational field trips. It is still operated by descendants of the Judd family, owners of the land for over 150 years.

Ahupua'a o Kualoa includes Kualoa Ranch, below the ridge, *mauka* of the highway, and Kualoa Regional Park, *makai* of the highway on the bay. The parklands were purchased by the City and County of Honolulu in 1972 for $8.5 million and have been on the National Register of Historic Sites since 1974. Excavations confirm the area as one of the important site complexes of ancient O'ahu. More than 16,000 artifacts have been recovered from the park site, including fishhooks, sinkers, *'ulu maika* stones, adzes, shell scrapers, worked bone, and dog tooth pendants, but continued work is needed to save further finds from beach erosion. Excavations at Kualoa have uncovered 75 human remains and the only physical evidence of a ritual pig burial used to mark an *ahupua'a* (district) boundary. Kualoa was at one time called Palikū, meaning "upright cliff." *(6/90–92; 28/180–181, 185–186, 188)*

30 *Mokoli'i (Chinaman's Hat)*

Small offshore island

LOCATION: **Off the eastern shore of Kualoa Regional Park. It is possible to visit the island with the aid of a kayak or flotation device, but not in Kona weather (people have been blown out to sea). Wading is not recommended, due to sharp coral, dangerous currents, and changing tides.**

Hi'iaka, Pele's sister, is responsible for Mokoli'i Islet, the sea stack just offshore from Kualoa. Commonly referred to as Chinaman's Hat, because of the similarity in shape to the Asian hats worn by immigrant workers on the 19th-century sugar plantation in the area (note the old sugar mill ruins beside the highway at the entrance to Kualoa Ranch), legend tells that it is the site of a mythic struggle and the remnants of a gigantic *mo'o* dragon.

Hi'iaka saved the neighborhood of Kualoa by slaying a threatening *mo'o*, Mokoli'i, and setting its huge flukes in the water as a landmark. In the heat of battle, Hi'iaka called on Pele for help, and was sent a smokey black cloud, charged with lightning to blind and strike down the *mo'o*. Mokoli'i, described in some tellings as a male, in others as a female creature, collapsed in defeat. Hi'iaka spread out the enormous lizard-like body of the beast to form the lowlands below the Ko'olau Mountain Range at Kualoa to provide travelers with a broad, flat pathway running through the area.

Following the harrowing battle, Hi'iaka chanted in triumph:

Kānehoalani lifts the sky;
Mokoli'i swims in the ocean—
The first-born child of Ko'olau—
A legion of fiends is Ko'olau,
Eager for mischief, subtle of trick.

The highest peak on the ridge overlooking Kualoa is known as Pu'u Kānehoalani, named for the father of Pele, a god who "ruled the heavens."

As mentioned in Site 28 and 29, Kamehameha III sold Kualoa and the island of Mokoli'i, including all the adjoining fishing grounds, in 1850 for $1,300. A bargain price, even in those days! *(6/91; 13/114; 20/167; 26/154; 28/180–182)*

III. North Shore

Huilua Fishpond at Kahana Bay.

The area referred to here as the North Shore includes the districts of
Koʻolau Loa ("long windward side") and Waialua, the entire northern
part of the island from Kaʻaʻawa in the east to Kaʻena Point in the
west.

It is along the North Shore that the famous big winter surf
rolls onto beaches known today as Sunset, Pipeline, and Waimea,
homes to numerous surfing competitions. But this area is also the
least densely populated, has the least industrial-commercial development, and sees less of the tourist traffic common to other places
on the island. The North Shore area is mostly agricultural land and
military reserves consisting of open land and forests.

This area has many sacred stones such as Kauhiʻīmakaokalani
(the Crouching Lion), Kahikilani (the Washington Stone), Pele's
Followers, Pōhaku Lānaʻi, and out at Kaʻena Point, Leina A Ka ʻUhane,
the leaping place for the souls of the dead.

Across the highway from the Kahikilani (Site 33), at Sunset
Beach, are the Paumalū petroglyphs. Originally there were as many
as seventy figures, mostly of humans and dogs, carved on a sandstone
ledge at sea level, just north of Kālunawai Kaʻala Stream. Unfortunately,
these petroglyphs are usually under sand, except when heavy storm
conditions substantially alter the beach. (3/97)

The two accessible fishponds on the North Shore are Huilua at
Kahana and Loko Ea in Haleʻiwa. They are both easily viewed from the
main road.

The island's largest existing *heiau* is Puʻu o Mahuka, a National
Monument and State Historic Place at Pūpūkea on the North Shore.
Other less accessible Waialua *heiau* ruins are Mōkaʻena in Kuaokalā,
on the ridge overlooking Kaʻena Point (giving it the highest elevation of

Tradition tells that Kamapua'a, a *kupua* that could change his shape into a huge pig, created these uniquely grooved geological features in the cliff face at Sacred Falls, which today looks like a dugout canoe and is called Kaliuwa'a.

a *heiau* on O'ahu at 1,200 feet); Kalakiki in Kamananui, a Registered Historic Place; Kohōkūwelowelo in Kawailoa, a supposed *kāhuna* monastery which was *kapu* to commoners; and Kupopolo, also in Kawailoa, which is on both the state and national registers of historic places and linked to the *kahuna* Ka'ōpulupulu. The restored Hale o Lono Heiau in Waimea Valley is very accessible.

Some other temple sites in the Ko'olau Loa district of northern O'ahu that are listed on the state register of historic places are Nīoi at Lā'ie, a place of human sacrifice; Hanawao in Punalu'u, subsequently used as a cemetery; and a number of unnamed sites in Ka'a'awa. Many other ancient rock structures in varying degrees of ruin could be added to this list.

A great number of burial caves can also be found in the cliff walls and canyon bluffs of the North Shore's terrain, with over 130 documented sites existing in Waimea Valley alone. These cave sites are *kapu* and are not accessible to visitors.

Another now-inaccessible site is Sacred Falls State Park in Kaliuwa'a Valley, associated with the Hawaiian demigod Kamapua'a. The valley trail to the 80-foot falls and pool features numerous natural landmarks that recall the pig god's adventures. Various wet patches along the stream and many unusual rock formations beside the trail denote events or beings described in the Kamapua'a mythology. Perhaps the most intriguing part of his story is how he saved his family from Chief 'Olopana. Kamapua'a and his family were chased back into the valley by the warriors of the chief and with no way out, Kamapua'a turned himself into a gigantic boar so that his family could climb one by one up his bristly back and over the *pali* to safety. His grandmother, Kamaunuaniho, insisted on climbing up his front, as was befitting one her age. In turning around and scraping his back up against the mountainside, Kamapua'a created the uniquely grooved and tough-like cliff face, which today looks something like a dugout canoe (*wa'a*). Unfortunately, Sacred Falls State Park has been closed since the tragic rockfall of Mother's Day, May 9, 1999, in which eight people died and fifty were injured. (The State of Hawai'i is deliberating whether or not to reopen the park to the public.) *(20/290–291; 28/162–164)*

Another state park, this one easily accessible, is Mālaekahana State Recreation Area, a former *pu'uhonua* (place of refuge). Here where *kapu* breakers formerly found forgiveness and amnesty, visitors still find refuge at the locally-run, 37-acre wooded beach park and gated campground. (Friends of Mālaekahana, 56-335 Kamehameha Hwy, Laie, HI 96762; (808) 293-1736, malaekahana@hawaii.rr.com)

Map of North Shore

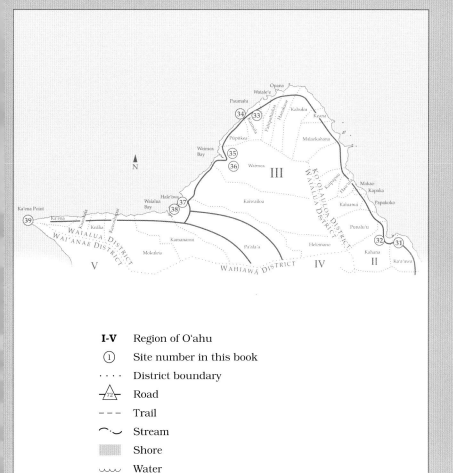

I-V	Region of Oʻahu
①	Site number in this book
· · · ·	District boundary
⚠︎72	Road
– – –	Trail
⌒‿	Stream
▨	Shore
∿∿∿	Water

31 *Kauhiʻīmakaokalani* (The Crouching Lion)

Rock formation on ridge

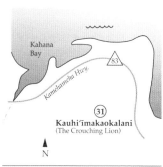

Kauhiʻīmakaokalani
(The Crouching Lion)

N

LOCATION: **On the ridge above Māhie Point, along Kamehameha Highway, at Kahana Bay (behind and above the Crouching Lion Restaurant). The formation is easily seen from the highway.**

Along Puʻuomāhie ridge in Kahana is the well-known Crouching Lion. This is the *kupua* or shape-changer, Kauhiʻīmakaokalani, who came to the north shore of Oʻahu from Kahiki at the same time as Pele's Followers (Site 34) and was apparently a relative of Pele. When Hiʻiaka passed this way on her journey around Oʻahu, she chanted to this rigid creature:

Kauhi, thou watch-tower of heaven,
Ensconced in the zigzag fluted wall—
Slipp'ry to climb as Kaliuwaʻa,
Or the struggling Puna-Hilo hills...
Thy body lies smothered in ferns...
Awake, thou explorer of heaven!
Awake, thou sender of Winter's rain...
The time of arising has come!

Kauhiʻīmakaokalani wished to follow Pele's beautiful sister, but he had turned to stone and could only struggle out of the heavy rock ridge to a crouching position. Hiʻiaka must have thought it best to let sleeping dogs lie, for a large-headed dog is what the Hawaiians saw in this rock formation. The idea of a lion was obviously introduced by Westerners sometime in the 19th century. There is also a turtle behind Kauhi on the ridge.

Somewhat further along the ridge to the north is a *pali pōhaku* called Palani. Palani was a local chief who, while surfing with his wife one day, was greeted by the goddess Hiʻiaka. Not knowing who she was, he answered rudely and was thereupon turned to stone. A large stone in the water at Kahana Bay is also called Palani. *(6/91–94; 26/92; 28/173–174)*

32 *Ahupua'a o Kahana*

Land section, enclosed pond, and fishing shrine

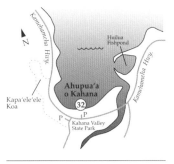

LOCATION: **52-222 Kamehameha Highway (83). The fishpond is visible on the south side of the bay. A 1/4-mile hike leads from the park restrooms to Kapa'ele'ele Ko'a and Keaniani Kilo, via the old railroad right of way (first right beside the former visitors' center, then after 100 yards take the forest trail to the left heading east along the north ridge). The loop trail returns to the highway near the public boat ramp.**

PHONE: **(808) 587-0300**

Ahupua'a o Kahana State Park is a 5,228-acre land division that includes a beach and bay, a fishpond and stream, forested and mountainous areas. It is the only publicly owned *ahupua'a* on O'ahu and is one of the wettest areas on the island with a 300-inch average annual rainfall at Pu'u Pauao, the valley's highest peak (2,670 feet). Kahana is based on the idea of a living park where the 140 Hawaiian residents are seen as personnel of the historic and cultural park setting.

It is at Kahana that some of the earliest dated remains have been discovered on O'ahu. Archaeologists have found evidence of human occupation here as early as AD 150. Of the archaeological sites in the park, Huilua Fishpond is the most accessible and most visible. It is said to have been built by Menehune, and is recognized as a National Historic Landmark. Originally, Huilua was a brackish pond fed by a number of freshwater springs as well as by Kahana Stream and the ocean. These conditions were ideal for raising *'ama'ama* (mullet) and *awa* (milkfish). The pond was rebuilt after a series of tidal waves damaged it in 1923, 1946, and 1957, but following a tsunami in 1960 the outer wall was broken and has not yet been repaired, although restoration has been done on part of the wall to bring it back to its original height and width. Huilua Fishpond is easily visible at low tide.

There are three *ko'a* (fishing shrines) in Kahana: Kapa'ele'ele Ko'a, Palani Ko'a, and Kauinie Ko'a. Kapa'ele'ele means "black kapa," and this accessible shrine was a place for offerings to Lono, a god noted for wearing a black *kapa* cape. Above the road on the north side of the bay, the shrine was associated with the promotion of *akule* (scad fish), and measured 24 feet by 14 feet. The site has been neglected in recent years and part of the northern side of the shrine has slid down the slope. Associated with this *ko'a* was Keaniani Kilo, a lookout above the *ko'a* where the *konohiki* would spot shimmering schools of *akule* swimming into the bay. Keaniani means "sparkling," and *kilo* means "lookout." Pu'u Kilo was a lookout spot on the other side of the bay, and was used in the morning and Keaniani Kilo was used in the evening. Also above the road, on the south ridge, used to stand Pu'u Makāne Heiau, a small temple probably devoted to agriculture and aquaculture.

In the late 1800s, the O'ahu Railway and Land Company operated a spur line here between the Kahana Plantation and the Kahuku Sugar Mill. In the 1940s, the U.S. military used the valley for jungle training. Subtle reminders of both activities can still be seen in Ahupua'a o Kahana. *(13/75; 20/164–165; 28/170)*

Kapa'ele'ele ("black kapa") is a fishing shrine and place for offering to Lono, a god noted for wearing a black *kapa* cape. Above the road on the north side of the bay, the shrine was associated with the promotion of *akule* (scad fish), and measured 24 feet by 14 feet, but has been neglected in recent years and part of the northern side of the shrine has slid down the slope.

33   *Kahikilani* (Washington Stone)

Upright rock formation

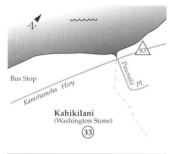

Kahikilani
(Washington Stone)
(33)

LOCATION: **Kahikilani can be seen from the bus stop across from 59-236 Kamehameha Highway, between Paumalū Place and Sunset Beach Elementary School. It is along the ridge above Paumalū Gulch.**

This *pōhaku* is named for Kahikilani, a legendary young Hawaiian surfer who came to the north shore of O'ahu from Kaua'i. Seeking adventure, each day he asked the sea birds where the most challenging surf could be found. One day the birds brought Kahikilani a *lehua lei* and told him of Ka'iulani, a beautiful maiden who sent the wreath with her love. Kahikilani went to her cave and there they were betrothed. Every morning thence, Ka'iulani gave Kahikilani a *lehua lei*, and he would return to their cave after surfing, still wearing the *lei*. One day, however, he headed home wearing strands of golden *'ilima* which a girl had given to him on the beach. Ka'iulani, on seeing this, was very angry and called on her *'aumākua* to punish him. Walking up the hill toward their cave, he paused to look back at the surf one last time and was suddenly turned to stone.

In more recent times, the story of Kahikilani has faded and an apparent resemblance to the first president of the United States has left the natural feature with the name Washington Stone. At one time, a Hawai'i Visitors Bureau sign along the highway helped to locate the "statue," but the sign has been removed and the stone is now overgrown and difficult to spot from the road. *(20/151–152; 26/64; 28/146–147)*

34 Pele's Followers

Several standing stones on an 'a'ā lava shelf at water's edge

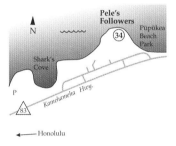

LOCATION: **On Kulalua Point, at Pūpūkea Beach Park. The site can be approached from Shark's Cove by walking over the sharp lava shelf, or from the Kahikilani side by walking along the sand beach.**

Tradition has it that these *pōhaku* were followers of Pele, the volcano goddess. She turned them to stone in order that they might become immortal, thus guarding the beach at Pūpūkea forever.

Paka'a, his wife Hina Alualumoana, and their sons Kuapaka'a, Ka'alenui, and Ka'aleiki are five of the followers of Pele. Holoholoua and Holoholomakani are the names of two others, boys who were like the rain and the wind in their quarreling. 'O'opuhalako'a is the eighth *pōhaku*.

Most of the stones average a height of ten feet with the tallest standing fifteen feet above the *'a'ā* lava shelf. *(20/151; 28/145)*

35 *Pu'u o Mahuka Heiau*

Stone temple enclosure

LOCATION: Pu'u o Mahuka Heiau is perched on the sloping promontory east of Waimea Bay in Pūpūkea, at an elevation of about 300 feet. Take Pūpūkea Road *mauka* from Kamehameha Highway until you come to the site entrance on your right.

Believed to have been constructed by Menehune, Pu'u o Mahuka ("hill of escape") is associated with the 18th-century *kahuna* Ka'ōpulupulu, and the O'ahu chief Kahahana. It was at this heiau that the great *kahuna* communed with the *akua* (god) Mahuka and ascertained that the Kaua'i chief Kekaulike desired peace with the O'ahu chief. Signal fires were used as visual communication between this *heiau* and the sacred complex at Wailua on Kaua'i. Pu'u o Mahuka Heiau was connected in its function with the slightly smaller Kupopolo Heiau located across Waimea Bay on private land. Pu'u o Mahuka was also believed to have been an advantageous place for chiefesses to give birth.

In 1794, three of Captain Vancouver's men sent ashore as a watering party from the *Daedalus* were taken in a skirmish with native warriors, and at least two of them were reportedly offered here at this *luakini heiau. Pahupū* warriors, tattooed over half their bodies and even on the insides of their eyelids, fell upon the unlucky foreigners. In 1795, when Big Island chief Kamehameha I conquered O'ahu, his high priest Hewahewa carried out religious ceremonies at this *heiau*. Then in 1819, a year before the New England missionaries arrived in

Hawai'i, all the images at this site were ordered destroyed by Kamehameha II.

Measuring 575 feet by 170 feet, and consisting of three adjoining enclosures, Pu'u o Mahuka is the largest *heiau* on O'ahu. A low surrounding stonewall, one to six feet in height, denotes the perimeter of the original temple platform. Probably built in the 1600s, the lower rock enclosures were a likely 18th-century addition. The *heiau* was paved with waterworn pebbles from Waimea Stream below. The altar area of the *heiau* is located within the larger, uppermost enclosure at the southern end, and to this day offerings are left by Native Hawaiians. The 2-acre *heiau* is set within the 4-acre Pu'u o Mahuka Heiau State Monument, which was declared a National Historic Landmark in 1962. Poised on the hilltop that overlooks spectacular Waimea Bay, this sacred Hawaiian site was an important feature in the social, political, and religious landscape of Waimea Valley and the entire North Shore. *(14/37; 20/147–150; 26/204; 28/142–144)*

Pu'u o Mahuka is the largest *heiau* on O'ahu, measuring 575 feet by 170 feet, and consisting of three adjoining enclosures. A low surrounding stonewall, 1 to 6 feet in height, denotes the perimeter of the original temple platform. The *heiau* was paved with waterworn pebbles from Waimea Stream below and the altar area is located within the larger, uppermost enclosure at the southern end of the 4-acre State Monument and National Historic Landmark.

36 *Ahupua'a o Waimea* *(Waimea Valley)*

Botanical park with waterfall and renovated ancient structures

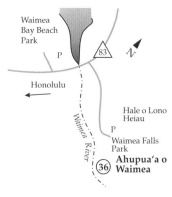

LOCATION: **59-864 Kamehameha Highway, Hale'iwa, across from Waimea Bay Beach Park.**

PHONE: **(808) 638-7766**

WEBSITE: **www.waimeavalley.net**

HOURS: **9 a.m. to 5 p.m., daily. Closed on Thanksgiving, Christmas, and New Year's.**

ADMISSION: **Adults $13; children & seniors $6. Resident & military discounts available.**

Waimea Valley is an *ahupua'a* (land division from mountains to sea) that has been occupied for at least a thousand years. The valley was a favored location for *ali'i* residence, and Hewahewa, Kamehameha I's trusted *kahuna*, made his home here. After being a privately-owned theme park and botanical garden for many years, it became the property of the Office of Hawaiian Affairs in 2006; this was following community protests that battled to keep the 1,875-acre valley from being developed for luxury homes.

Beside the entrance building, at the back of the parking lot, is restored Hale o Lono Heiau. This small temple has been renovated, complete with a replica of a thatched *mana* house, drum house, oracle towers, and a small wooden image of Lono. Its facing wall was discovered in 1974, excavations began in 1982 and were completed in 1987. Dedicated to Lono, this multi-terraced temple was an agricultural-class *heiau* consecrated to the promotion and growth of flora in the region. Branch coral built into the terraces was gathered alive from deep waters and thus could be carbondated from the time it died. These dates suggest the *heiau* could have been in use as early as AD 1000–1100. During restoration, the original postholes were found and reused to support the *'ohia* logs of the present towers. A pit at the site contains the partial remains of a likely high-

Inside the park, house sites and living quarters were uncovered and stabilized in 1972. This living compound is called the *kauhale*, "eating house" complex. Some of the excavated home sites have been restored with *pili*-grass huts to simulate their possible appearance at the time of their use (ca. AD 1000–1100).

ranking chief as an offering to Lono. Hale o Lono can be viewed year round (without an admission fee to the park).

Inside the park proper, agricultural terraces have long been visible, but it wasn't until 1976 that house sites and living quarters were uncovered and stabilized. This living compound is called the *kauhale*, "eating house" complex. One excavated stone platform contained two burials, leading park archaeologists to believe it was a burial temple or a high chief's residence. Some of the excavated home sites have been restored with *pili*-grass huts to simulate their possible appearance at the time of their use (ca. AD 1000–1100). An *ahu pōhaku*, or "heap of stones," was discovered among the excavations and is thought to have marked the entrance to a chief's residence. Ancient Hawaiians left ti leaves at such a place as a special recognition and offering of peace. A stone was placed on the leaf to prevent it from blowing away. All that remains of these old offerings today are the stones, but it was the offering connected with the ti leaf which was important. The deliberate pile of stones at the *kauhale* may have also marked the place of a Makahiki tribute.

Today, the agricultural terraces in the valley are utilized by the Waimea botanical gardens, and special features such as sweet potato rock mounds have been restored and planted as they were in ancient Hawai'i. Archaeologists have also examined some 138 burial caves and shelters tucked into the canyon walls. All these caves are *kapu* to visitors. Excavations in the valley are ongoing.

Waimea Valley, formerly known as Waimea Falls Park, is presently managed by Hi'ipaka LLC, a non-profit organization. The park provides free, guided tours as well as a brochure with map to the ancient sites and the botanical gardens. There are more than 5,000 species of tropical plants in the valley, and Kamananui Stream, together with Waihi (Waimea Falls) is home to four of the five native freshwater fish in Hawai'i. *(28/130–132)*

37 *Loko Ea Fishpond*

Enclosed pond

LOCATION: *Mauka* side of Kamehameha Highway 83, just past the Hale'iwa Boat Harbor Bridge, next to Jameson Restaurant. May be viewed from the highway.

Loko Ea, or Lokoea, consists of three bodies of water making up a productive fishpond system over a 6.75-acre area. A freshwater spring that originates at an upwelling by 'Uko'a Fishpond, just upstream, flows down and feeds a small side pond called Keiki Pond, continues into a side channel that connects to the ocean, and also flows into the major pond, Loko Ea. Loko Ea is a *pu'uone*, meaning "pond near shore," and is part of a tributary system that runs into Waialua Bay by way of a saltwater channel.

Hawaiian tradition speaks of runners that carried freshly caught, still wriggling fish across the islands for the benefit of *ali'i*. During the reign of the great O'ahu chief, Kakuhihewa, his runners were said to be able to compass the island twelve times in a day. This chief apparently loved Loko Ea for its *'ama'ama* (mullet). In fact it was said that the "Mullet God" lived at this pond. Stories of strange occurences and bizarre-looking fish were told about this pond and 'Uko'a Fishpond. Large white fish would lead others to be harvested, but it was understood by the *konohiki* that these white fish were never to be caught and eaten. The Hawaiian historian Kamakau writes of Laniwahine, the *mo'o* of 'Uko'a Fishpond, and fishermen still claim to see this pond spirit as a beautiful figure out in the water or witness the unusual effects of her deeds.

Loko Ea belonged to a long succession of *ali'i* including Queen Ka'ahumanu, Kamehameha III, Victoria Kamāmalu, Ruth Ke'elikōlani, and Princess Bernice Pauahi Bishop. Queen Lili'uokalani was a frequent visitor to the pond in the late 19th century, as she had a summer home here, and her favorite swimming hole bordered the fishpond.

In the 1960s, the original 2.4-acre Loko Ea was dredged to make the present, deeper (1 to 4 feet), three-pond complex. It has two *mākāhā*. The fishponds and most of the land in Hale'iwa are now the property of Kamehameha Schools. There is a $4.5 million development plan for the entire area that includes pond renovation and management upgrades. *(20/142; 28/119–120; 30; 32)*

Loko Ea belonged to a long succession of *ali'i* including Queen Ka'ahumanu, Kamehameha III, Victoria Kamāmalu, Ruth Ke'elikōlani, and Princess Bernice Pauahi Bishop. Queen Lili'uokalani was a frequent visitor to the pond in the late 19th century and her favorite swimming hole was beside the fishpond.

38 Pōhaku Lāna'i

Coral outcropping

LOCATION: **Along the west side of Kaiaka State Recreational Area, not far from Kaiaka Bay. Drive to the loop and park. The site is to the left.**

This natural monument, reminiscent of a dolmen, consists of two limestone formations: the lower one, a rock mound about 6 feet high, the upper an oval slab balanced like a mushroom cap upon the lower. The two reach a combined height of about 12 feet. Pōhaku Lāna'i, measuring 93 feet in circumference, is an unusual outcropping; there is nothing like it in the region.

Local tradition says it was used as a lookout for fishermen. When the *kilo i'a* (fish-seer) spotted a school of fish, he would beat the roof rock with a wooden club, which would sound an echoing tone like that of a bell stone (such were common elsewhere in the islands). This sound would alert other fishermen in the area.

It is said the stone floated across the Pacific from Kahiki, and out of respect for its origin, chiefs would consult the local god who was worshiped at Pōhaku Lāna'i. This site is associated with offerings of prayer, particularly the special request that the chief would stand invincible in battle. Lāna'i, as used here and in the name of the island, may mean literally "day conquest."

Pōhaku Lāna'i, once thoroughly overgrown by vegetation, can now easily be found just beyond a clearing in the southwest corner of Kaiaka State Recreational Area. Several banyan trees have recently been trimmed from the *pōhaku*; their stumps still cling to the coral mound. *(20/140–141; 28/113–114)*

39 *Ka'ena*

Cape of land

**LOCATION: At the end of
Farrington Highway 630.
Requires a minimum two-hour
roundtrip hike from the end of
the road; best done with water,
hat, and sunscreen. Sometimes it
is partially accessible by 4-wheel
drive vehicles. Ka'ena Point State
Park may also be approached
from the Wai'anae coast on the
Leeward side of the island.**

Ka'ena means "the heat" or "red hot," and as the western-most point of O'ahu, within Ka'ena Point State Park, it can certainly get hot here, especially on a summer afternoon. Ka'ena is said to be named for a relative of Pele who accompanied her from Kahiki and decided to make this place his home. On her mythic journey around O'ahu, Hi'iaka, Pele's younger sister, comes to this place and chants:

> Ka'ena, salty and barren,
> Now throbs with the blaze of the sun;
> The rocks are consumed by the heat,
> Dappled and changed in their color...

It is also said that the demi-god Māui stood at Ka'ena when he attempted to fish Kaua'i closer to O'ahu. (On a clear day, the Garden Isle can be seen from here). Using his magic fish-hook Manaiakalani, Māui snagged the base of the distant island and pulled with all his might. In one telling of the story, helpers did not follow instructions to look away, but turned to see the magic feat, thereby breaking the spell. The hook released itself from the bulk of Kaua'i, but brought with it a small piece of the island that dropped into the waters off Ka'ena Point. This rock, Pōhaku o Kaua'i, can still be seen today as the furthest rock to the northwest of O'ahu. A rock closer in to the point is called Pōhaku

Leina A Ka 'Uhane, a large limestone outcropping, known as "the soul's leaping place," was also known as White Rock, Kahuna's Leap, and Ghost's Leap. Ancient Hawaiians held the belief that when a soul leaves the body at death or near-death it travels west in the direction of the setting sun. This was the leaping place of souls for the island of O'ahu.

o O'ahu. When Māui's fishhook let go of Pōhaku o Kaua'i, it had such momentum that it snapped back across O'ahu as far as Pālolo Valley, where it struck the Ko'olau Mountains with such force that it carved out Ka'au Crater at the back of the valley. While on her travels through Ka'ena, Hi'iaka addressed this very stone, Pōhaku o Kaua'i—said by some to be Pele's father—asking for a canoe to help her and her party reach Kaua'i.

Ancient Hawaiians, as other indigenous peoples, held the belief that when a soul leaves the body at death or near-death, it travels west in the direction of the setting sun. Ka'ena was known to be a place where a wandering soul sought out its 'aumakua in order to either be directed back to its body, if its time had not yet come, or to the *leina a ka 'uhane* (leaping place of souls), where it would jump off into *pō*, the deep darkness of the spirit world. Every island had such leaping places, and Hawai'i Island had one in every district. Leina A Ka 'Uhane, a large stratified limestone outcropping, known as "the soul's leaping place" for O'ahu, was also known as White Rock, Kahuna's Leap, and Ghost's Leap.

Looking up at the ridge from Leina A Ka 'Uhane, it was possible to see a broad, sandy swath cut through the vegetation and rocks, from sea to mountaintop (no longer so visible). This trail marked where, after being caught by a mighty *kahuna*, a gigantic fish called Kumunuiakea, was dragged to a *heiau* on the summit. The great fish was cut into many small pieces and when waters rose in a legendary deluge, all the pieces became the *kumu* fish that then populated Hawaiian waters.

From Ka'ena Point, a 59-acre Natural Area Reserve, one sees both the northern and southern coastlines, with waves coming in from opposite directions. It is like looking back on the island from another world. One may experience from here the *wahi pana* of this special place, and the great *mana* of O'ahu. (3/134–136; 6/100–108; 20/124–127; 28/92–95)

IV. Central Oʻahu

Kūkaniloko, "the birthplace of *aliʻi*," is one of the most sacred places on Oʻahu and is considered the *piko* (navel) of the island.

The Central region of Oʻahu includes Wahiawā and part of the ʻEwa district north of Pearl Harbor. Its main feature is the rich, mostly agricultural land lying between the Waiʻanae and Koʻolau mountain ranges. This central plain, known as Leilehua Plateau, was formed when the two volcanic mountain ranges joined.

Captain George Vancouver made the following observations concerning Central Oʻahu while anchored at Pearl Harbor's West Loch in 1793: "The part of the island opposite to us was low, or rather only moderately elevated, forming a level country between the mountains that compose the east [Koʻolau] and west [Waiʻanae] ends of the island. This tract of land was of some extent but did not seem to be populous, nor to possess any great degree of natural fertility; although we were told that, at a little distance from the sea, the soil is rich, and all the necessaries of life are abundantly produced."

Today, Central Oʻahu land supports a wide spectrum of uses, from large conservation and forest reserves, diversified agriculture, to populated commercial areas, residential developments, and military bases.

The Kūkaniloko *pōhaku* were arranged in two rows of eighteen lava rocks facing north and flanking a central birthing stone. The stones, many of which are indented with bowl-like shapes, now lie haphazardly in a small grove of coconut and eucalyptus trees.

Almost all of the dozens of fishponds and fishtraps that once were in and around Pearl Harbor have been destroyed for the military's use of waterways. Remnants of two fishponds that are no longer functioning and not listed as specific sites here are in the West Loch of Pearl Harbor, and serve as freshwater wetlands for endemic, endangered Hawaiian waterbirds. These ponds are part of Pearl Harbor National Wildlife Refuge.

The most important sacred site in Central O'ahu is certainly Kūkaniloko, "the birthplace of *ali'i*." The nearby Ho'olonopahu Heiau (now destroyed) served Kūkaniloko and housed the ritual drums of 'Ōpuku and Hāwea that were used to announce the birth of *ali'i*. This site is considered the *piko* (navel) of the island.

More than fifteen *heiau* structures are known to have been located in this central area of O'ahu. The only partially restored and maintained site in the area however, is the peaceful Keaīwa Heiau, a medicinal temple, at the top of 'Aiea Heights.

A *pōhaku* site that is not included here because of its inaccessibility is called the O'ahunui Stone, and is shaped like the island of O'ahu. In the 1890s, people from Honolulu would ride out to the stone and walk around it so they could tell others they walked around O'ahu. O'ahunui was also the name of a local chief, who was killed by his sister for cannibalizing her two sons and was turned to stone. There are a number of important sacred stones that can be seen in this area including Hūpēloa, the Healing Stones of Wahiawā, and the above mentioned Kūkaniloko.

Map of Central Oʻahu

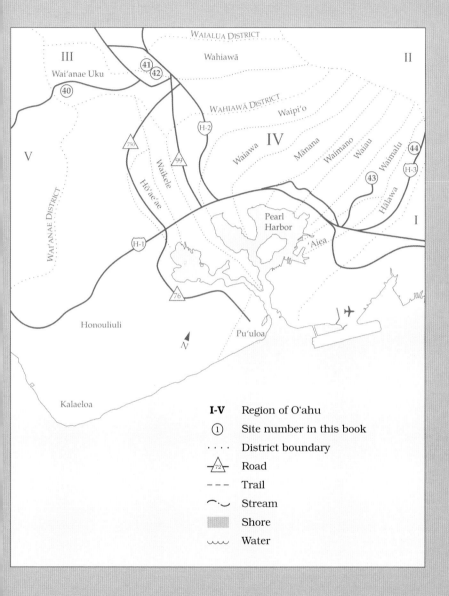

I-V   Region of Oʻahu

①   Site number in this book

· · · ·   District boundary

Road

– – –   Trail

Stream

Shore

Water

40   *Hūpēloa*

Large boulder

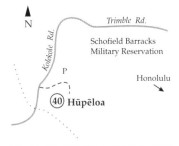

LOCATION: **At the end of a short, steep trail atop Kolekole Pass Road, on the windward side of the military checkpoint. Military ID or special permission is required to visit this site, as it can only be reached from Schofield Barracks Military Reservation or Naval Magazine Lualualei. Ask for permission at the main gate.**

Pōhaku Hūpēloa is an impressive boulder measuring five to six feet high and eight feet wide, with a lip-like formation extending about one and one-half feet out from the rest of the stone. The bowl-like depression holds rainwater and may have been used for offerings.

Oral tradition has it that Hūpēloa, which stands just to the side of an ancient trail, represents the female guardian of the pass, named Kolekole. Kolekole means "to strip the flesh," and that may have been a practice of the Hawaiian martial arts warriors who were said to lie in wait for travelers at the top of Kolekole Pass in order to practice their skills in *lua* fighting (dislocating joints and breaking bones).

A more recent interpretation is that this *pōhaku* was a sacrificial stone whose bowl was designed to catch blood from human sacrifices. It is said that *kāhuna 'anā'anā*, or black magicians, who had become something of a detriment to the community were beheaded at this site. Although ancient Hawaiians made both human and animal sacrifices, there is no evidence that they ever made blood sacrifices. *(7/22–23; 20/134; 28/134)*

41 *Kūkaniloko*

Numerous boulders

Kūkaniloko
(41)

N

Wahiawā

LOCATION: **Between Wahiawā and Haleʻiwa. Off Kamehameha Highway opposite the road to Whitmore Village, in a field, amongst coconut and eucalyptus trees.**

This is the first ancient site on Oʻahu to have been officially recognized, preserved, and protected, thanks to the efforts of the Daughters of Hawaiʻi in 1925. It is the birthplace of high-ranking *kapu aliʻi.*

The site is believed to have been established by chief Nānākāoko and his wife, Kahihiokalani. Their son, Kapawa, tops the list of important *aliʻi* born here. Kapawa is the legendary chief who was overthrown by Pāʻao, the Tahitian *kahuna* who is believed to have introduced human sacrifice to Hawaiʻi. Other important *aliʻi* born here were Kākuhihewa and Laʻa. Holoholokū, at Wailua, Kauaʻi, is another sacred birthing place.

The Kūkaniloko *pōhaku* were arranged in two rows of eighteen lava rocks facing north and flanking a central birthing stone. The stones, many of which are indented with bowl-like shapes, now lie haphazardly in a small grove of coconut and eucalyptus trees. According to Hawaiian tradition, *ʻaumākua* inhabited the stones and could relieve the pains of labor and ease the birthing process. The birthing ritual conducted at this site involved the participation of thirty-six chiefs, who stood by as the *aliʻi* mother reclined on a central stone called Kūkaniloko. *Kapu* drums announced the birth as the newborn was quickly taken to the nearby Hoʻolonopahu Heiau

At certain times of year, shadows fall across petroglyphs of concentric circles on one of the stones at Kūkaniloko, indicating a connection to solar observation at the site.

(now destroyed) for the ceremonial cutting of the umbilical cord. The two ritual drums were called by name, 'Ōpuku and Hāwea. An *ali'i* born at Kūkaniloko was guaranteed to be "a chief divine: a burning fire." Kamehameha the Great (chief of the Big Island) had hoped his *kapu* children by his highest-ranking wife would be born at Kūkaniloko, but each time his wife Keopuolani was unable to travel to O'ahu.

It is reported that the sacred stones of Kūkaniloko are aligned with many other important places on the island, and there are claims of astronomical significance as well. The stones at the site are shaped by wind, rain, and water erosion, and look like mythic models of miniature islands with their own little mountain ranges. In fact some say that Kūkaniloko was a former navigational training school and the scattered stones, once in a different arrangement, represented the various islands of Polynesia. One particular stone is thought to represent the island of O'ahu, and it casts shadows from its outer ridges (said to be aligned to peaks on the Ko'olau and Wai'anae ranges) across a series of engraved concentric circles at certain times of the day and year creating a sundial effect. Kūkaniloko is refered to as the *piko* (navel) of the island, and as a sacred birthing place, a stellar navigational center, and a possible solar observatory, it is clearly a *wahi pana* of particular power and importance, a place of great *mana*. (7/16–21; 12/50–64; 20/134–137; 28/138–140)

42 *Healing Stones of Wahiawā*

Two standing stones

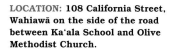

LOCATION: 108 California Street, Wahiawā on the side of the road between Ka'ala School and Olive Methodist Church.

One of the two Healing Stones of Wahiawā is 5 feet tall, 2 feet wide, and shaped like a tongue. The other stone stands about three feet high and has the shape of a shoe (part of the stones are buried underground). The larger stone is called Pōhaku Hoʻola Kino, "rock that gives health to the body." It is also called Keanianileihua o Kalani and was known for its miraculous healing powers. The name of the smaller rock is unknown, but oral tradition holds that both stones were originally one stone that broke in two.

In the late 19th century, prompted by a dream in which the spirit of the stone addressed him, an Irish rancher by the name of George Galbraith moved the stone from a riverbed to a clearing at Kūkaniloko, where it drew many Hawaiians who experienced its curative powers. Pilgrims flocked to the sacred stones, offering prayers and gifts, and the stone was moved to a cemetery in Wahiawā, a mile away. However, the next day it appeared back at its original location. It was moved again, and again it somehow returned, people said, on its own. A third time it was moved in a wagon from which it fell and broke in two. The two stones now remained at the spot where they were placed, and became even more popular. People commonly draped the healing stones with *lei*, and left food, candles, photographs, Chinese prayer-papers, and money. In 1927 as much as $1,000 a month was left at the site. This money went to neighborhood road improvements and a parking lot for visitors.

After the outbreak of World War II, visitors to the *pōhaku* site decreased, in part due to various measures imposed by the federal and local governments. In 1948, a Japanese crypt-like shelter was built over the stones, and in the 1990s a Hindu structure was erected as the stones were worshipped as a manifestation of Shiva. The former cemetery is now a suburban housing development, and the Healing Stones of Wahiawā are visited by the faithful of various religions, as well as by curious tourists.

Another Hawaiian legend tells of two sisters from Kaua'i who by means of supernatural power could fly to O'ahu, but only during the dark of night. On their last such flight, they were struck by the first rays of morning sunlight, turned to stone, and fell into a streambed near Kūkaniloko, the sacred birthplace of chiefs. These sisters are said to be the two Healing Stones of Wahiawā. *(7/8–12; 28/141)*

The larger of the two Healing Stones of Wahiawā is called Pōhaku Ho'ola Kino, "rock that gives health to the body." It is also called Keanianileihua o Kalani and was known for its miraculous, healing powers.

43 Keaīwa Heiau

Rock wall enclosure

Keaīwa Heiau (43)

'Aiea Heights Dr.

'Aiea

Ulune St.

Moanalua Rd.

Halawa Hts. Rd.

H-1

LOCATION: Off Moanalua Road, at the top of 'Aiea Heights Drive, inside Keaīwa Heiau State Recreation Area.

Keaīwa means "mysterious" or "incomprehensible" according to one interpretation, and may also be the name of an early priest who had mysterious healing powers. Another translation of the word is "a period of fasting, prayer, and meditation." The Keaīwa site is now known to have been a *heiau ho'ōla*, an ancient medicinal center served by *kāhuna lapa'au*. These medicine men and women would have engaged in "... fasting, prayer, and meditation" as part of their training and healing practices. The ways by which the *kāhuna lapa'au* diagnosed and treated patients with medicinal plants from the surrounding herb gardens were probably considered by lay persons to be "mysterious" and "incomprehensible"—hence, there are reasons for the name Keaīwa.

Perhaps one of the most mysterious of the *kāhuna* practices relates to the picking of plants. Certain plants were picked only with the right hand; these were considered under the rulership of the god Kū. A gathering chant to Kū would name the part of the plant to be picked as well as the patient for whom it was intended. It would then speak of the other parts of the plant and its legendary home in Kahiki. *Kāhuna* preferred to pick medicinal herbs early in the morning to avoid chance

Keaīwa Heiau is planted with an exhibition garden of medicinal plants and is located in a beautiful 384.5-acre state recreational area, Keaīwa Heiau State Park. The *heiau* measures 100 feet by 160 feet and has three-foot-high walls in places. Much of its rockwork was carried away prior to rededication of the *heiau* in 1951, and some of the curved arrangement of stones may be fairly recent. A moderate 4.3-mile loop trail is also featured in the park.

encounters with people that might cause unfavorable omens. Also, the vitality of a plant was understood to be at its highest during the morning hours and this diminished as the sun reached its zenith and began to wane. Therefore gathering was often done from the east side of the plant, from the side of the rising sun. Other flora was under the guardianship of the goddess Hina (associated with the moon), and along with the proper ceremony, could be picked only with the left hand and from the west.

Keaīwa Heiau was probably built at the time of Kākuhihewa, a 16th-century chief. It is planted now with an exhibition garden of medicinal plants and is located in a beautiful 384.5-acre state recreational area. The *heiau* is at an elevation of 1000 feet above sea level and its enclosure, which is just a small part of the original temple, measures 100 feet by 160 feet and has three-foot-high walls in places. Much of its rockwork was carried away prior to rededication of the *heiau* in 1951, and some of the curved arrangement of stones is recent. *(8; 20/103; 26/101; 28/11–12)*

44 Hālawa-Luluku Interpretive Development Area

Natural and archaeological features

This site includes North Hālawa Valley in Central O'ahu, and Ha'ikū Valley, Luluku agricultural terraces, and Kukui o Kāne Heiau on the Windward side. These areas were impacted by construction of the controversial interstate highway, H-3, the largest public works project undertaken by the State of Hawai'i, at a cost of $1.3 billion. The 16-mile long freeway, the most expensive stretch of roadway in the world ($100 million per mile), destroyed numerous archaeological features in its path even though it is mostly elevated and was redesigned to avoid sensitive sites. Archaeological surveys of the area were not completed at the time of design and construction, and in fact, some reports were not completed until years after the highway was opened. H-3 was originally planned to go through Moanalua Valley (Site 11) but was shifted to Hālawa Valley because of Moanalua's cultural significance. The project was begun in 1987 and was completed in 1997. A total of 70 archaeological sites were identified in the highway corridor and more than 61,000 artifacts were recovered.

CONTACT: **Hālawa-Luluku Interpretive Development Project, 677 Ala Moana Blvd. Suite 811, Honolulu, HI 96813.**

PHONE: **(808) 594-0282**

WEBSITE: **www.hlid.org**

The North Hālawa Valley portion of this area is bordered by 'Aiea Ridge to the north, North Hālawa Ridge to the south, and the Ko'olau Range to the east. The valley opens to Pearl Harbor in the west. Pre-contact agricultural, habitation, burial, and religious sites have been found in North Hālawa Valley, particularly Hale o Papa, a women's religious site, and a possible *luakini heiau*. Some smaller features discovered in the valley were a *pueo* (owl) rock, a *honu* (turtle) rock, a *mano* (shark) rock, and a Portuguese brick oven. It has been suggested in reports that 68 of the 70 sites brought to light in the area may be eligible for nomination to the National Register of Historic Places.

The *'ili* (small land division) of Ha'ikū is in the *ahupua'a* (larger land division) of He'eia, and is now connected to Hālawa Valley by way of the H-3 tunnel. The vertical cliffs define the amphitheater shape of the valley with its highest peak, Pu'u Keahiakahoe, summitting at 2,750 feet. A 1930s survey of the area found six *heiau*, a burial cave, and two religious shrines among other features in the valley. The U.S. military took control of most of the valley between 1942 and 1972, greatly restricting access. The valley was then turned over to Coast Guard use of an Omega Navigational Transmitter Station (because of the valley's ideal open dish-shape) that operated until 1997, when it became obsolete and H-3 was opened.

The *'ili* Luluku with its agricultural terraces, located in the *ahupua'a* of Kāne'ohe, were cultivated in taro like much of their neighbor district of Ha'ikū. The terraces are located on the eastern base of the Ko'olau Mountain Range at an elevation between 62 and 716 feet, in the midst of the H-3 Kāne'ohe Interchange. Divided by Likelike Highway and overgrown with banana, these terraces originally provided the setting for *kalo* (taro) production, and were in use as such until the early 20th century. Other archaeological features such as boundary walls, stone platforms, burial sites, a "sentinal rock," and a petroglyph rock have also been noted in this area.

However, the most significant site in this area is that of Kukui o Kāne Heiau. This site is on the boundary of Luluku and Punalu'u Mauka. Surveys from 1915 and 1930 mentioned the precise location of the *heiau*, but a 1985 testing survey for the interstate designated the site in question simply as agricultural terraces. A controversy over this interpretation ensued as H-3 went into construction and archaeologists, polititians, and community groups took sides on the issue. This site, apparently a complex of four sites, was believed to be the largest temple in the Ko'olau Poko district, and radiocarbon dates of AD 915 and 1200 have been recorded in the area. However, a final report from the contract archaeologists concerning interpretation of this site has only recently appeared and has not yet been made public.

The Hālawa-Luluku Interpretive Development working group is charged with preserving and educating people about the cultural and natural landscape of the area affected by the construction of H-3. Some of their goals are to implement actions to restore and stabilize cultural sites, provide access to the sites and develop interpretive programs and educational materials, maintain the ecological balance of the area's environment through knowledge and practice of Native Hawaiian culture. For information about the sites and accessibility of project areas contact the working group through their website. *(28/9)*

V. Leeward Side

The coastal rock outcrop of Mauna Lahilahi in Mākaha reveals a number of petroglyphs.

The Leeward side of the island stretches from Barbers Point, including part of the 'Ewa district, to Ka'ena Point, encompassing the entire Wai'anae coast. The Leeward district of O'ahu is the dry side of the island, so named because it lies in the lee of the southwestern Wai'anae mountain range.

Industrial, commercial, and residential development in the Barbers Point region ('Ewa district) continues to expand with the development of a so-called "second city," much to the misfortune of ancient sites in the area. A large portion of this district is uplifted coral reef with natural sink holes, which the ancient Hawaiians used for various purposes, both sacred and mundane. Many early artifacts have been excavated in this neighborhood, including stone tools, fishhooks, and human and animal bones.

Along the Wai'anae coast to the north is Kū'īlioloa Heiau at Pōka'ī Bay and Kamaile Heiau on a ridge above Mākaha Valley. Back in the same valley is Kāne'ākī Heiau, a restored and accessible temple that served the entire Wai'anae coast in ancient times. Other important *heiau* sites that have not been included in this guidebook because of their present inaccessibility are: Pūnana'ula Heiau in Wai'anae, Ukanipō Heiau in Mākua (this site is sometimes made accessible by the military, which leases the area for $1 a year until 2029 for use as a live firing range), and Laukīnui Heiau in Mākaha (said to have been constructed by the Menehune). Punapōhaku complex is another ancient

In Mākua Valley, a restricted military live firing range, there are many archaeological features, including *heiau, ahu*, agricultural terraces, and this petroglyph rock that depicts numerous dog and human figures. Access to the sites is periodically made available.

Hawaiian site of important archaeological significance for the Leeward side.

A noted natural feature at Mākaha is Mauna Lahilahi, which if you don't see "you haven't seen Wai'anae."

The most accessible and impressive cave on O'ahu is Kāneana at Mākua. The beach almost directly across the road from Kāneana is 'Ōhikilolo, also known as Barking Sands. The latter name derives from the sounds the sands make when trod upon in dry weather (July through September). It is here along the Leeward coast that some of the most beautiful and least crowded beaches on O'ahu are found.

To explore a bit further, and truly get off the beaten path, drive to the end of the road, park at Yokohama Beach Park, and walk out to Ka'ena Point State Park by following the jeep trail. The coastal track winds past a small cave and out to the westernmost point of the island. This is another approach to Ka'ena (Site 39) and the small rock islet known as Pōhaku o Kaua'i said to have been pulled over to O'ahu from Kaua'i by the demigod Māui. Also here at Ka'ena Point is the rock called Leina A Ka 'Uhane, where oral tradition tells that the souls of the dead leap over into the spirit world. The view looking back at O'ahu from Ka'ena Point is like looking back at the earth from the vantage point of another world.

Map of Leeward Side

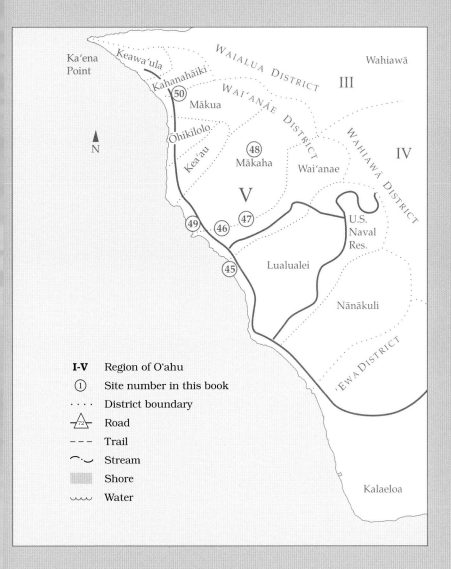

Ka'ena
Point

Keawa'ula

Kahanahāiki

(50)

Mākua

'Ōhikilolo

Kea'au

WAIALUA DISTRICT

WAI'ANAE DISTRICT

Wahiawā

III

WAHIAWĀ DISTRICT

IV

(48)
Mākaha

Wai'anae

N

V

(49) (46) (47)

(45)

Lualualei

U.S.
Naval
Res.

Nānākuli

'EWA DISTRICT

Kalaeloa

I-V   Region of O'ahu

(1)   Site number in this book

· · · ·   District boundary

(72)   Road

– – –   Trail

   Stream

   Shore

   Water

45   *Kū'īlioloa Heiau*

Terraced stone structure

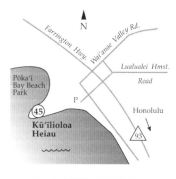

This *heiau* is perched at the tip of Kāne'īlio Point and surrounded on three sides by water. The original construction included three platforms, the main one faced the open ocean at the *makai* end of the point, the others faced Pōka'ī Bay and Mikilua Beach, respectively.

Kū'īlioloa means "the long dog Kū," so the *heiau* was apparently named for a legendary dog (like the *kupua* dog of Nu'uanu Valley) who protected travelers. Some negative qualities were associated with this dog, and according to one story, he was defeated by the pig god, Kamapua'a, in a contest at Kualoa (Site 29).

Kū'īlioloa Heiau was also said to be a temple of learning and training. It has been suggested that the skills taught might have related to fishing and the various arts and crafts of the sea.

The site commands a beautiful view of the ocean, the Wai'anae coastline, and the Wai'anae mountain range. It is located in a public park and maintained by the State of Hawai'i. *(20/112; 26/120; 28/69)*

Kūʻilioloa Heiau is surrounded on three sides by water and includes three terraced platforms facing the open ocean at the *makai* end of the point. It was believed to be a temple of learning and training, related to fishing, navigation, and the various arts and crafts of the sea.

46 *Kūka'au'au Cave*

Natural rock feature

LOCATION: At the base of Kamaile Ridge above the water pumping station, between Mākaha and Wai'anae. To get to the cave requires a five-minute uphill hike from the end of Kauawaha Road or from the dog-leg turn in Māiu'u Road, off Farrington Highway.

This cave's location, between Kamaile Heiau (Site 47) and a once large Hawaiian settlement in Mākaha, may have suited it for special ritual functions, but it is not known to have been a place of burial, as so many caves were. At a minimum, ancient Hawaiians used it for shelter, as one post-Western contact interpretation of its name suggests, *kuka* meaning "coat." *Kūkā*, with the macrons, means to discuss or consult, and *'au'au* means to swim or bathe. Whatever its function may have been, the close proximity to Kamaile Heiau suggests that Kūka'au'au had a religious significance of some kind.

The cave faces due south, toward the ocean; its entrance is approximately 10 feet high and 25 feet wide. Today, however, it is somewhat concealed by a large *kiawe* tree, some *haole koa* bushes, and tall grass. The cave goes in about 40 feet and has a dirt-fill floor. From its mouth, there is a commanding view of the coast.

Directly below Kūka'au'au is the Kamaile spring, also known as Keko'o, the most important ancient water source for the area. *(20/114–115; 28/73)*

47 *Kamaile Heiau*

Single terrace temple platform

Kamaile Heiau
(47)
Kūka'au'au
Cave

Pumping
Station

N

Honolulu →

LOCATION: On Kamaile Ridge, above Kūka'au'au Cave and the pumping station, between Mākaha and Wai'anae. Visiting the heiau involves a 20-minute steep, uphill climb with no marked trail.

Kamaile Heiau was built above Kūka'au'au Cave (Site 46), at an elevation of 400 feet, on Kamaile Ridge. In comparison to other ancient temples on O'ahu, it is a medium-sized *heiau*, and although built on large basalt rocks, its facing is carefully fitted and unusually even in places. The open terrace measures 60 feet across and 134 feet in length and once had four small rectangular enclosures running lengthwise along the platform. This *heiau* at one time served a large Hawaiian settlement in the Mākaha area, and along with Mauna Lahilahi, marks the boundary between Mākaha and Kamaile *ahupua'a*. It is also known by the name Kamaile 'Unu, and is considered of the *luakini* class. Its location affords an exceptional view of the Wai'anae district, Mākaha Valley, and the Leeward coastline. *(20/114–155; 28/73)*

The rock foundation of Kamaile Heiau provides a majestic view of the ocean and the Mākaha area. It is aligned with Mauna Lahilahi and marks the boundary between Mākaha and Kamaile *ahupua'a*.

48   *Kāne'ākī Heiau*

Enclosed stone platforms

LOCATION: **Take Mākaha Valley Road, past the golf course, to Ala Holo Loop in upper Mākaha Valley. There is a guard station where one must check-in.**

HOURS: **10 a.m. to 2 p.m., Tuesday through Sunday, weather permitting.**

Kāne'ākī Heiau is one of the most captivating temples on the island. Situated just above a valley stream in a lush forested area, the atmosphere at the site is moody and intense.

Kāne'ākī is known to have been both an agricultural *heiau* in its early days and later a war temple. According to radiocarbon dating, construction of the agricultural *heiau* began ca. AD 1545 with a two-terrace structure. Further construction phases followed, eventually more than doubling the *heiau* size by AD 1650. The final stage included the addition of the largest platform, a *papahola*, and shows the influence of a paramount chief in Mākaha Valley, during whose time Kāne'ākī became a *luakini heiau* (human sacrifice temple).

The upper stone platform today displays a restored thatched *hale mana* (house of spiritual power), *hale pahu* (drum house), a wooden *lele* (offering stand), two wood frame *'anu'u* (oracle towers), and a small, carved image of the god Kū. The offering stand would receive bananas, coconuts, roasted pig, and in some cases, humans as sacrifice. The *papahola* is the large, lower platform where wooden god images were placed for certain ceremonies, an indication of a *luakini heiau*. Behind the *heiau*

Kāneʻākī Heiau, seen from the *papahola*.

proper is Hale o Papa, a house where religious services were held for women.

Kāneʻākī literally means "hair-switch-man," possibly in reference to the god of fresh water, Kāne. However, *kī* is the word for the ti plant, a plant attributed to Kū. So Kāneʻākī could mean "man of the ti," in honor of Kū (who was also associated with agriculture). Evidence from extensive excavations has led archaeologists to believe that the *heiau* first served the god Lono, a god of agriculture and peace, and later was rededicated to Kū, a god of agriculture and war.

Kamehameha the Great at one time quartered his army in Mākaha, poised to attack Kauaʻi. It is believed Heaʻaheaʻa, *kahuna* to Kamehameha, used Kāneʻākī as a war temple then, in order to help unite the islands. Kauaʻi, however, was not to be taken by force, as bad weather and illness among the troops of Kamehameha thwarted the attack. Later, a peaceful agreement was reached between Kamehameha and the paramount chief of Kauaʻi regarding rulership of the islands.

Kāneʻākī Heiau is now owned and maintained by Honolulu Federal Savings and Loan and is open throughout the year. Call Maunaʻolu Estates Security at (808) 695-8174 for confirmation of visiting hours before planning a trip. Nearby Makaha Resort & Golf Club (84-626 Mākaha Valley Road) often offers guided tours. Call for further information at (808) 695-9544. *(13/117–119; 20/119–120; 28/77–78, 84)*

49   *Mauna Lahilahi*

Small coastal mount

**LOCATION: Adjacent to Mauna
Lahilahi Beach Park and
approached from Lahilahi Place
off Farrington Highway.**

Mauna Lahilahi means "thin mountain," and
although it is considered part of Mākaha, it is
actually a dividing marker, together with Kamaile
Ridge, of the *ahupua'a* of Mākaha and Kamaile. It
is said that if you have not seen Mauna Lahilahi,
then you have not seen Wai'anae. Tradition refers
to it as the eyes of Wai'anae and its 230-foot
summit provided a good lookout point for spotting travelers passing through the area. It is said
that robbers used it for this purpose, letting
groups pass by, but descending upon weak or
individual wayfarers.

However, according to local tradition,
Mauna Lahilahi was originally a site sacred to the
god, Kāne. Many place names in this area
acknowledge Kāne, and he is still greatly revered
by Hawaiians in Wai'anae. Stories connecting
Papa, as mother earth, and Wākea, the sky father,
to this place are still told by local *kūpuna*. It is
also said that the fish god Ai'ai marked this place
as a prime fishing spot.

At the eastern end of Mauna Lahilahi are numerous dog and human petroglyph figures. Abraded into the coastal cliff rock they add further significance to the *wahi pana* of this site.

There are numerous ancient rockwall enclosures, small stone platforms, several shrines, and a possible *heiau* site at Mauna Lahilahi. There are also burial sites, and more than two dozen petroglyphs are abraded into rocks on the 11.145-acre peninsula. According to local tradition the peak holds astronomical significance, particularly in recognition of the summer solstice. Archaeological surveys and radiocarbon dating show this area was in use from at least ca. AD 1300.

In 1793, British Captain George Vancouver noted in his logbook that he sighted in this area "a high rock remarkable for its projecting from a sandy beach." Clearly, Mauna Lahilahi was meant. Mauna Lahilahi Beach Park is to the east of the mount, and Turtle Beach is to the west. Shark Island, the large rock just offshore from Mauna Lahilahi, is said to be the mother, the other scattered rocks, its children. *(3/144–146; 15; 28/77)*

50   *Kāneana* (Makua Cave)

Natural feature

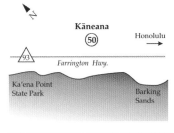

Kāneana
(50)   Honolulu →

Farrington Hwy.

Ka'ena Point
State Park   Barking
                              Sands

LOCATION: **On the *mauka* side of Farrington Highway, visible from the road, north of Kahuakauila Stream.**

At least two interpretations are possible for the name Kāneana. *Ana* means "cave," but *Kāne* could refer to the Hawaiian god or simply to "man" in general. Thus Kāneana is the "cave of the god Kāne" or "the cave of man."

Also known as Mākua Cave, Kāneana was the home of a legendary shark goddess who held sway in the waters off Ka'ena Point. Entering the cave by way of a sea entrance, the goddess would emerge from the cave in the shape of a woman and lure unsuspecting victims back to Kāneana. Some stories speak of the shark god's son, a half-fish, half-human *kupua* (shape changer).

In the early part of the 20th century, Kāneana was still considered *kapu* by Mākua residents, even though performance of ritual functions in the cave had ceased the century before. Local elders then recalled how in ancient times *kāhuna* conducted ceremonies around a sacrificial altar paved with coral stones and lit by the dim light of *kukui*-nut torches. Little else is recorded concerning the use of Kāneana Cave.

Kāneana or Mākua Cave in Wai'anae.

The cave is 35 feet high and 20 feet wide at its entrance and it has two passages, the deepest of which extends more than 100 feet in from the mouth. There is no apparent sea entrance to the present-day cave.

The sacredness of the site has greatly diminished, judging from the extensive graffiti spray-painted on the cave walls and the concrete barriers erected to prevent four-wheel drive vehicles from entering the antechamber.

The beach almost directly across from Kāneana is known as 'Ōhikilolo and, more commonly, as Barking Sands due to its unusual sounds at certain times of the year. The sand barks when walked across! Also nearby is Kea'au Park, where petroglyphs of a dog and several human figures are carved on a sandstone ledge. This ledge, however, is usually covered with sand. *(20/123; 26/84; 28/81–83)*

Appendix A

Selected Sites for Visitors

The following easy-to-find sites are recommended for visitors to Hawai'i who have only a limited amount of time in which to explore ancient O'ahu. There is no fee for any of the sites listed below, but transportation is essential.

Starting with the Wizard Stones (Site 1) in Waikīkī, head from there into town to see Ka Wai a Ha'o (Site 5) and right across the street, Pohukaina ('Iolani Palace Grounds) (Site 6).

Then, leaving Honolulu proper behind, get on H-1 eastbound, which turns into Kalaniana'ole Highway 72. Going through Hawai'i Kai, you'll see Maunalua and Paikō Lagoon (Site 12) on your right. Continue past spectacular Hanauma Bay (Site 14), well worth a more lengthy stop, and the Hālona Blowhole where you will then find on your left Kohelepelepe (Site 16), otherwise known as Koko Crater. Early morning light provides the best effect for viewing this *pali pōhaku* and, if you stop beside the highway just past Hawai'i Kai Golf Course, the best vantage point for viewing Kohelepelepe, you'll also get a good look at Kapaliokamoa (Pele's Chair) (Site 17) on the opposite side of the road.

Continue along Highway 72 past Sea Life Park and Pōhaku Pa'akikī (Site 18) through Waimānalo to Ulupō Heiau (Site 20). This journey takes you from East O'ahu to the Windward side, to just outside of Kailua town. From here you can see the Nu'uanu Pali Notches (Site 10) from a distance. When you have walked around and sufficiently taken in the *heiau*, return to Kalaniana'ole Highway 72 westbound and proceed to Kamehameha Highway 836 in order to see He'eia Fishpond (Site 26). Highway 836 becomes 83 in this vicinity, and proceeding northbound again you'll soon arrive at Kualoa Beach Park, where you can easily see Ahupua'a o Kualoa (Site 29) and Mokoli'i (Chinaman's Hat) (Site 30) by entering the park.

Still further north along Kamehameha Highway, you'll find Kauhi'īmakaokalani (Crouching Lion) (Site 31) marked by a Hawai'i Visitors Bureau sign just before the highway curves around Kahana Bay. Part of Kahana Bay reveals Huilua Fishpond (Site 32) at low tide. Once on the North Shore proper, find Pu'u o Mahuka Heiau (Site 35), the largest temple site on the island and one that affords spectacular views of the area.

You can see Hale o Lono Heiau (Site 36) at the entrance of Waimea Valley without leaving your car or having to pay admission. Just drive all the way to the back of the parking lot that is to the left and behind the entrance, restaurant, and shops. The *heiau* is behind a low fence, up against the hillside.

As you leave the North Shore and head toward Central O'ahu, stop at Kūkaniloko (Site 41) just before entering Wahiawā on Kamehameha Highway 80.

Then get on the H-2 freeway heading back toward Honolulu. This would normally be a very full day's traveling, but if you still have time and energy for the Leeward side of O'ahu, head toward Wai'anae when you get to the H-1 interchange. Seeing Kū'īlioloa Heiau (Site 45) on Pōka'ī Bay, Mauna Lahilahi (Site 49), and Kāneana (Mākua Cave) (Site 50), the latter two right beside Farrington Highway 93, will complete your introductory tour and give you a well-rounded impression of the various kinds of ancient sites that can be seen on O'ahu. However, it is best to read the various site descriptions and pick the sites to visit that most interest you.

Appendix B

Collections and Cultural Events

Local museums have collected many artifacts and assembled a good deal of information pertinent to the ancient sites on O'ahu. Their collections draw from the Hawaiian Islands as a whole, and from the entire Pacific region.

Bishop Museum's collection is the most extensive in the state and in America. In addition to its artifact collection and special exhibitions, this museum, located in Honolulu, has an extensive research library, and its educational and cultural departments sponsor numerous lectures, classes, and activities.

Bishop Museum
1525 Bernice Street
Honolulu, HI 96817

(808) 847-3511; www.bishopmuseum.org

HOURS: 9 a.m. to 5 p.m. Closed Tuesdays and Christmas Day.

ADMISSION: Adults $17.95, Seniors & Children $14.95

The Honolulu Academy of Arts also houses a quality collection of Hawaiian and Pacific Island artifacts in addition to their general art collection. The Academy features exhibitions, and sponsors lectures, workshops, and special events on Hawaiiana. Admission is free on the first Wednesday of every month.

Honolulu Academy of Arts
900 S. Beretania Street at Ward Avenue
Honolulu, HI 96814

(808) 532-8701; www.honoluluacademy.org

HOURS: Tuesday-Saturday, 10 a.m. to 4:30 p.m; Sunday, 1 p.m. to 5 p.m. Closed Mondays.

ADMISSION: Adults $10, Seniors & Children $5.

Another place worth visiting for its cultural events and replica historic displays is the Polynesian Cultural Center in Lā'ie, between Ahupua'a o Kahana (Site 32) and Kahikilani (Site 33).

Appendix C

Preservation

The ancient sites of O'ahu are cultural treasures and as such are invaluable to all people of all ethnic backgrounds, for all time. They provide spiritual inspiration as well as irreplaceable knowledge. The archaeological resources of all the Hawaiian Islands need to be protected against natural destructive forces as well as careless individuals and groups conducting vandalism or seeking short-term gain.

Since the Antiquities Act of 1906, numerous federal laws have been passed by the United States Congress to help protect and conserve the ancient sites located on public lands and reservations throughout America. The National Historic Preservation Act of 1966 is a particularly effective piece of legislation. As a result of this legislation, many sites have been listed on the national and state registers to secure official recognition of their significance as historic places and to aid in their preservation. Little actual protection is guaranteed these sites, however, unless they fall within special county-zoned districts or state conservation areas, and they are enforced.

None of the federal laws, nor similar state laws, can protect *all* sites, especially those on private property, where landowners may knowingly or unknowingly destroy important contextual evidence as well as valuable artifacts. Hawai'i state law requires site surveys of both public and private lands slated for development, but because developers hire the archaeologists, a conflict of interest may arise, even if only in theory. Therefore, even with the survey reviews provided by the State Historic Preservation Division of the Department of Land and Natural Resources, weak links in the preservation process can at times occur.

Public interest and understanding are necessary for any law to be truly effective. Each citizen has a role to play and must take at least partial responsibility for the preservation of ancient sites. Only through vocal support and local action can ancient sites be protected from not only natural deterioration, but also vandalism and rapid and sometimes thoughtless land development of the kind that has already devastated an estimated two-thirds of the known historic sites on O'ahu.

Several sites described in this book display the ways citizens have shown complete disregard for the ancient cultural treasures of Hawai'i: cave walls spray-painted with graffiti, petroglyphs cut away or painted over, stones from temple precincts rearranged or simply stolen, even structures built directly on top of ancient sites.

To combat further destruction of ancient Hawaiian sites, tour the accessible sites and educate yourself and others about them so that you and your family gain an understanding of the importance of such places. When you see preliminary signs of land use change or development, ask the landowner or the state if the site has been surveyed by an archaeologist. And, as the U.S. Park Service recommends when visiting an ancient site, take nothing but photographs and leave nothing but footprints.

Some organizations and agencies promoting the preservation of ancient sites of O'ahu are:

Historic Preservation Division
Department of Land and Natural Resources
State of Hawai'i
601 Kamokila Boulevard, Suite 555
Kapolei, HI 96707
http://hawaii.gov/dlnr/hpd/hpgrtg.htm

Society for Hawaiian Archaeology
P. O. Box 23292
Honolulu, HI 96823
www.hawaiianarchaeology.org

Historic Hawai'i Foundation
680 Iwilei Road, Suite 690
Honolulu, HI 96817
www.historichawaii.org

Appendix D

Hawaiian Pronunciation

Hawaiian is a lovely, melodious language. The alphabet comprises thirteen letters: seven consonants, *h, k, l, m, p, w,* and five vowels, *a, e, i, o, u.*

Pronunciation of the consonants is roughly similar to that of their English counterparts. The letter *w* is the most different. The *w* is usually pronounced like a *v* after *i* and *e,* and like a *w* after *u* and *o.* When *w* is the first letter, it can be pronounced either v or w.

All words end in a vowel and vowels are generously used, sometimes in surprising combinations by comparison to English usage. Many words consist solely of vowel clusters. Thus, the following sentence becomes possible in Hawai'i: *I 'Aiea i 'ai 'ia ai ia i'a.* (In [the town of] 'Aiea the aforementioned fish was eaten.)

Hawaiian vowels are generally pronounced as their equivalents in Spanish. However, with the addition of a glottal stop (written as a single open quote in front of a vowel: *'a*) or a macron (written as a horizontal line over a vowel: *ā*) the sound quality of the vowel changes.

The glottal stop is common in many Polynesian languages. It can be described as a momentary stoppage of the air flow passing through the glottis, producing a sudden small thrust of air, not unlike a tiny cough. The closest equivalent in English might be the catch of air in the utterance of "Oh-oh!" when something is amiss.

The macron doubles the sound length of a vowel.

The proper use of the glottal and macron is critical to correct pronunciation of Hawaiian words. Many words whose letter spelling is the same represent very different meanings depending on the presence or absence of these two marks:

kau	to place, put, hang, etc.
kāu	your, yours
ka'u	my, mine
Ka'ū	name of a district on the island of Hawai'i

—David Kāwika Eyre

Glossary of Terms

ahu	Heap, pile; altar, shrine.
ahupua'a	Land division running from mountain top to sea, formerly denoted by an *ahu* (heap) of stones or a pig burial.
akua	God, goddess, image, idol, spirit.
ali'i	Chief, chiefess, king, queen, royalty, nobility, aristocrat.
'anu'u	Ancient *heiau* tower.
'aumakua	Ancestral spirit or personal god. (Pl.) *'aumākua*.
'awa	Narcotic drink made from a plant root of the same name.
hale	House, building, home, place.
Hawai'i	The island group as a state; also, the largest and most recently formed island of the group.
heiau	Hawaiian temple, place of worship or offering; stone platform or earth terrace.
heiau ho'ōla	Ancient medicinal center.
Hi'iaka	Sister goddess to Pele.
hōlua	Sled, ancient wooden sled used on grassy slopes.
Honolulu	Sheltered bay. Capital city of the State of Hawai'i.
'ili'ili	Pebble, small stone.
'ilima	Native shrub. Official flower of O'ahu.
Kaho'olawe	Name of one of the Hawaiian islands.
Kahiki	Legendary island home of the ancient Hawaiians; thought to be Tahiti.
kahuna	Priest, shaman, expert. (Pl.) *kāhuna*.
kāhuna 'anā'anā	Black magicians.
kāhuna lapa'au	Medicine men and women.
kai	Sea water, salt water.
kalo	Taro, a tuber crop used to make *poi*, a Hawaiian staple.
kama'āina	Child of the land, native-born, familiar; now commonly used to mean long-time resident.
Kamapua'a	Pig god.
Kamehameha	Name of a line of Hawai'i Island chiefs/monarchs.
Kanaloa	God of the oceans.
kāne	Man, male, husband. (Cap.) God of fresh water.
kapu	Taboo, forbidden, sacred, consecrated.
Kaua'i	Name of one of the Hawaiian islands.
kauhale	Plural of "house"; group of houses comprising a Hawaiian home.
ki'i	Image, statue, picture.
ki'i pōhaku	Stone image, petroglyph
ko'a	Fishing shrine; coral; coral head; fishing grounds.

koko	Blood.
Kona	Leeward sides of the Hawaiian islands.
kōnane	Ancient game resembling checkers.
konohiki	Owner of fishing rights
Ko'olau	Windward sides of the Hawaiian island; also, the eastern mountain range on O'ahu.
kū	To stand; stop. (Cap.) God of war.
kupua	Shape-changing being; demigod.
kū'ula	Altar or stone used to worship or attract fish or fish gods.
Lāna'i	Name of one of the Hawaiian islands.
lapa'au	Medical practice; to heal, cure.
lehua	Red flower of the native *'ōhi'a* tree. Official flower of the island of Hawai'i.
lei	Flower garland.
Lono	God of agriculture.
lua	Hawaiian martial arts.
luakini	Hawaiian temple where ruling chiefs prayed and human sacrifices were offered.
Mākaha	Land area on Leeward O'ahu; fierce.
mākāhā	Sluice gates used in fishponds.
Makahiki	(Cap.) Ancient festival beginning about mid-October and lasting four months. Sport and religious festivities are conducted at this time and war is *kapu*.
makai	Toward the ocean.
mana	Spiritual, divine, or miraculous power.
Maui	Name of one of the Hawaiian islands.
Māui	Name of a demigod.
mauka	Toward the mountains.
Menehune	Legendary race of small people who worked at night during prehistoric times building temples, roads, fishponds, and other structures.
Moloka'i	Name of one of the Hawaiian islands.
mo'o	Mythological lizard, reptile, dragon, merman or mermaid-like creature functioning as guardian of a body of water.
mō'ī	King, sovereign, paramount ruler.
O'ahu	One of the Hawaiian islands.
Pā'ao	10th-century Tahitian (?) *kahuna* believed to have brought a colony to Hawai'i, and to have introduced human sacrifice.
pahu	Drum, box.
pali	Cliff, precipice.
papahola	Level pavement beside a *heiau*.
Pele	Volcano goddess.
pōhaku	Rock, stone.
pu'u	Any kind of protuberance, bulge, heap, pile, mound, hill, peak.
pu'uhonua	Place of refuge, sanctuary.
wa'a	Dugout canoe.
wai	Fresh water; any liquid other than sea water.

Selected Bibliography

1. Acson, V. 2003. *Waikīkī: Nine Walks Through Time.* Honolulu: Island Heritage Limited.
2. Beckwith, M. 1976. *Hawaiian Mythology.* Honolulu: University of Hawai'i Press.
3. Clark, J. R. K. 2005. *Beaches of O'ahu.* Honolulu: University of Hawai'i Press.
4. Cordy, R. 2002. *The Rise and Fall of the O'ahu Kingdom.* Honolulu: Mutual Publishing.
5. Cox, J. H., and E. Stasack. 1970. *Hawaiian Petroglyphs.* Honolulu: Bishop Museum Press.
6. Emerson, N. 1915. *Pele and Hiiaka: A Myth from Hawaii.* Honolulu: Honolulu Star-Bulletin Limited.
7. Gutmanis, J. (no date). *Pohaku: Hawaiian Stones.* Lā'ie, Hawai'i: Brigham Young University.
8. ———. 1994. *Kahuna Lā'au Lapa'au.* Honolulu: Island Heritage Publishing.
9. Handy, E. S. C., et al. 1970. *Ancient Hawaiian Civilization: A Series of Lectures Delivered at the Kamehameha Schools.* Vermont and Tokyo: Tuttle Co. Pub.
10. Kamakau, S. M. 1976. *The Works of the People of Old: Nā Hana a ka Po'e Kahiko.* Honolulu: Bishop Museum Press.
11. ———. 1991. *The Works of the People of Old: Nā Mo'olelo a ka Po'e Kahiko.* Honolulu: Bishop Museum Press.
12. Kawaharada, D. 1999. *Storied Landscapes: Hawaiian Literature & Place.* Honolulu: Kalamakū Press.
13. Kirch, P. V. 1985. *Feathered Gods and Fishhooks.* Honolulu: University of Hawai'i Press.
14. ———. 1996. *Legacy of the Landscape: An Illustrated Guide to Hawaiian Archaeological Sites.* Honolulu: University of Hawai'i Press.
15. Komori, E. 1987. *Archaeological Survey and Testing at Mauna Lahilahi.* Honolulu: Bishop Museum.
16. Kwiatkowski, P. F. 1991. *Na Ki'i Pōhaku: A Hawaiian Petroglyph Primer.* Honolulu: Ku Pa'a Incorporated.
17. Lee, P., and K. Willis. 1987. *Tales of the Night Rainbow.* Honolulu: Paia-Kapela-Willis 'Ohana, Inc.
18. Maa, T. L. 1988. *Kānāwai Mau Mo'olelo: Laws of Historic Preservation in Hawai'i.* Honolulu: Office of Hawaiian Affairs.
19. Malo, D. 1971. *Hawaiian Antiquities (Moolelo Hawaii).* 2nd ed. Honolulu: Bishop Museum Press.

20. McAllister, J. G. 1933. *Archaeology of O'ahu*. Honolulu: Bishop Museum Press.

21. McBride, L. R. 1969. *Petroglyphs of Hawai'i*. Hilo: Petroglyph Press.

22. Newman, T. S., et al. 1970. *Hawai'i Register of Historic Places: Bibliography of Hawaiiana*. Honolulu: Division of State Parks.

23. O'Connor, M. 1987. *A Walk into the Past: A Self-Guided Walk in Kamananui Valley of Moanalua*. Honolulu: Moanalua Gardens Foundation.

24. Okamoto, W. & Associates. 1996. *Ka Iwi State Park Master Plan and Final Environmental Impact Statement*. Honolulu: Department of Land and Natural Resources, State of Hawai'i.

25. Paki, P. 1972. *Legends of Hawaii: Oahu's Yesterday*. Honolulu: Victoria Publishers, Ltd.

26. Pukui, M. K., S. H. Elbert, and E. T. Mookini. 1966. *Place Names of Hawaii*. Honolulu: University of Hawai'i Press.

27. Sato, V. and C-S, Lee. 2007. *Keeper of Mōli'i Pond: An Informal Account of George Uyemura and His Amazing Hawaiian Fishpond*. Waimānalo: Oceanic Institute.

28. Sterling, E. P., and C. C. Summers. 1978. *Sites of Oahu*. Honolulu: Bishop Museum Press.

29. Stump, J. B. 1981. *Our Hawaii Kai: A History of Hawaii Kai and Maunalua*. Honolulu: n.p.

30. Summers, C. C. 1964. *Hawaiian Fishponds*. Honolulu: Bishop Museum Press.

31. Wisniewski, R. 1987. *Hawaiian Monarchs and Their Palaces (A Pictorial History)*. Honolulu: Pacific Basin Enterprises.

32. Wyban, C. A. 1992. *Tides and Currents: Fishponds of Hawai'i*. Honolulu: University of Hawai'i Press.